IMAGES
of America

CHICAGO'S
MOTOR ROW

ON THE COVER: Prospective customers line up for a test drive outside the Auburn-Cord dealership at 2401–2409 S. Michigan Avenue on Chicago's Motor Row around 1935. The Auburn Automobile Company of Auburn, Indiana, sold cars from this location from 1931 to 1936. (Courtesy of the David Kerr collection.)

IMAGES
of America

CHICAGO'S MOTOR ROW

John F. Hogan and John S. Maxson
Foreword by Jay Leno

ARCADIA
PUBLISHING

Copyright © 2021 by John F. Hogan and John S. Maxson
ISBN 978-1-4671-0762-4

Published by Arcadia Publishing
Charleston, South Carolina

Printed in the United States of America

Library of Congress Control Number: 2021947870

For all general information, please contact Arcadia Publishing:
Telephone 843-853-2070
Fax 843-853-0044
E-mail sales@arcadiapublishing.com
For customer service and orders:
Toll-Free 1-888-313-2665

Visit us on the Internet at www.arcadiapublishing.com

*In memory of my brother William H. "Bill" Hogan,
safe in the arms of the Lord, September 19, 2021*
—*John Hogan*

To Jennifer, Pres, Mollie, and Liz
—*John Maxson*

CONTENTS

FOREWORD

Reflecting on my early days working for a car dealership in the Boston area makes me appreciate what the business of selling cars must have been like a century ago. Chicago's Motor Row was a place where a person went to buy early cars and dream about how owning one would change their life. In fact, in those days, buying a car revolutionized the way people thought about nearly every aspect of their world.

When Motor Row's first dealership opened in 1905, only the wealthiest Americans could afford to own and drive automobiles. In fact, the cost of a car was roughly equal to what a typical worker earned for an entire year. But within a short time nearly any person with a decent job, a successful small business, or a good farm could afford a car, travel longer distances for shopping, enjoy a better job, visit friends and family more frequently, relax on a Sunday drive, and even work in the burgeoning automotive industry.

The region was a powerful economic engine for Chicago. It has been estimated that 116 different brands of cars were available for sale on Motor Row. The dealerships, maintenance, and repair shops and stores that sold tires, parts, and accessories employed thousands of Chicagoans, many of whom were African Americans and recent European immigrants. For these families, Motor Row changed the way they lived, in many cases elevating them into America's growing middle class with opportunities for better housing, education, and recreation.

Just visiting Motor Row during its heyday, generally considered to be 1905–1936, must have been an experience. Seeing the dramatic buildings by world-famous architects and showrooms with brand new Packards, Pierce-Arrows, and Pierces amidst ferns and exciting art dazzled crowds of curious visitors. It was a place the whole family could dress up for and, at no cost, visit for an afternoon of delight, wonder, and amazement.

Dealerships were different then. Palatial structures with finely inlaid floors and high ceilings supported by columns made the would-be buyer feel like a king. And dealers knew the high value their customers placed on traditional values like honesty and integrity. To combat customers feeling that they were the victims of over-charges and tricks like setting back odometers, dealers often played the role of evangelists, refusing to sell a coupe to an unmarried man without the car being fitted with a chaperone seat. This small stool was installed on the passenger side so a suspicious father at least had the opportunity to ride along with his daughter on dates. And business was different. At first, factories didn't offer warranties; dealerships did. Warranties were a dealership's way of securing a relationship and the best hope for having customers return for repairs and maintenance.

Marketing was also different. For example, the Detroit Electric, a popular brand of battery-powered cars, was marketed specifically to women because all it took was the flip of a switch to drive to a friend's home or go shopping downtown. No cranking, choking the engine, retarding the spark, and all that. In fact, Henry Ford's wife, Clara, drove a 1914 Detroit Electric until the 1930s, way past the time when battery-powered cars were popular.

And steam-powered cars were important, marketed to those who enjoyed power, speed, and novel technology. By 1906, one third of the cars were electric, one third were steam-powered, and one third were powered by internal combustion engines. Cadillac introduced the electric starter in 1912, other manufacturers followed, and the dynamics changed.

Marketers knew that showing women driving cars in ads continued to be important for three reasons: ads encouraged women to buy the cars themselves; ads empowered women so they could influence their husbands regarding which car to buy; and showing women driving cars in ads demonstrated to everyone how comfortable, well-styled, and easy to operate the car must be.

The second and third African American dealerships in America were in Chicago (sorry Chicago, Kansas City had the first). Black entrepreneurs Kenneth Campbell and Thomas Brown opened a Hupmobile dealership in 1928. Dan Gaines followed with his dealership in 1936. Mr. Gaines used the advertising slogan "The only Ford-Lincoln-Zephyr dealer owned and operated by race personnel." As African Americans became more affluent, the automobile became a critically important tool for access to better jobs, better housing, better schools for their children, and a more leisurely lifestyle.

While early cars set many trends, there are several that didn't stick. For example, early Fords, Franklins, and a few others offered a mother-in-law seat, a small open chair-like structure outside the car's body. I doubt many mothers-in-law actually rode in this seat, but the name was catchy. Some car owners felt more secure if their mechanic rode along, another use for a small seat outside the car. Hood ornaments were popular, both as a factory item and after-market accessory. Since many of these miniature chrome or nickel statues were of lovely ladies in various degrees of nudity, I am sure that the phrase "But it came with the car" was common around the homes of new car owners. Another short-lived accessory was Woodlites, easily the coolest looking headlights available, but with a drawback: the glow of a fine cigar was brighter. Finally, the total loss chassis lubrication system enabled a driver to pump oil to springs and other suspension components before each drive. The downside was that overflow oil dripped to the pavement and left six or eight sizeable puddles to be stepped in by pedestrians. None of these innovations survived.

The year 1926, near the peak of Motor Row's popularity, is significant because that is when the number of automobiles in America had grown to match the number of horses and mules, about 20 million of each. After that, the number of horses continued to decline and, in part due to dealerships like those on Motor Row, the number of cars skyrocketed. Not only did the cars become more sophisticated mechanically, but they became more important in American life. For farmers, cars and light trucks became essential. For city folks, the car was a convenient way of placing oneself in society. Of course, cars had a utility, but owning a luxury car translated to the owner's concern for elegant styling, skilled craftsmanship, and mechanical superiority. Similarly, owning a well-maintained and clean basic practical car labeled a person as true to the values of America: hard work, economic efficiency, and financial security.

All this is to say that Chicago's Motor Row was much more than a place to buy a car. It was the place where dreams were made and people celebrated the freedom to come and go on a magic carpet of steel, glass, and rubber.

I applaud the auto enthusiasts who campaigned hard to secure Motor Row's landmark status and salute the Commission on Chicago Landmarks and the National Historic Landmarks Committee for certifying that this classic automobile history deserves and requires protection. May we look to the future with the same high regard for quality, innovation, and styling that those who visited Chicago's Motor Row saw a century ago and celebrate this place where dreams came true.

Jay Leno
May 19, 2021

ACKNOWLEDGMENTS

Chicago's Motor Row celebrates the union of vintage automobiles with classic architecture. The authors have been fortunate to obtain the help of individuals with expertise in both fields as well as others with the varied skills to make us look good, or at least better than we deserve. One of the funniest people in America also happens to be one of the most knowledgeable about classic autos, so we were understandably excited when Jay Leno agreed to write the foreword. Two more vintage car collectors with extensive knowledge, Bob Joynt and Dr. Herb Lederer, provided valuable insights, as did Dave Kerr, who wrote his master's thesis on Motor Row. Bob and Dave helped lead the fight to place Motor Row in the National Register of Historic Places. A short walk from Motor Row is historic Glessner House, whose executive director, Bill Tyre, was especially generous with his time and image collection. The former longtime editor of the *Auburn (Indiana) Evening Star*, Dave Kurtz, shared photographs of the cars that put his lovely city "on the map" and continue to draw visitors to its first-rate auto museum. Carla Watson Owens delivered research as well as historical images and Matthew Owens provided artwork, for which we are indebted. Additionally, auto aficionados Gene Maslana and Mike Roach assisted with research. Thanks to *Chicago Tribune* reporter Ryan Ori for sharing his insights into the future of Motor Row. Our editor-in-chief, Judy Brady, kept the project on track every step of the way, and finally thanks to our Arcadia editor, Caroline (Anderson) Vickerson, for her guidance.

INTRODUCTION

Legendary Chicago fire chief Jim Horan, according to a possibly apocryphal story, set out in the early 20th century to buy the fire department's first piece of motorized equipment. The vehicle was to be the chief's command car or buggy, a term that endured well into the mechanized era of firefighting. A horse lover, Horan said he felt sorry for any animal that had to pull a buggy carrying his 250-pound frame. The chief and his two drivers visited an upscale but otherwise unidentified auto dealership, quite possibly the Winton establishment at Fourteenth Street and Michigan Avenue. For some unknown reason, they felt ignored by a salesman, so they took their business to a dealership nearby. That was how a 1906 Buick became the first motorized vehicle of the Chicago Fire Department.

This supposed incident, part of department lore, could serve as a template for the way consumers could and did shop for cars in Chicago over the next 30 years. If a customer didn't like what he saw or the way he was treated at one dealership, he could go next door, down the street, or several blocks away. If he still couldn't find what he was looking for, in all likelihood, the vehicle didn't exist. That was the rationale behind Motor Row, sometimes called "Automobile Row," a car shopping corridor along S. Michigan Avenue stocked with as many as 116 different makes offered at 65 salesrooms.

The district stretched roughly from Twelfth to Twenty-Sixth Streets and was dedicated almost exclusively to automotive sales, service, and repairs. This novel marketing concept earned Motor Row Chicago landmark status in 2000 and an entry in the National Register of Historic Places in 2002. The latter distinction places it in the company of Mount Vernon, Pearl Harbor, and about 2,600 other sites recognized as "historic places that hold national significance," according to its administrator, the National Park Service. In formulating the 28-acre district, mapmakers included nearly all buildings within its boundaries, regardless of the type of business—a few goats interspersed with the sheep, in so many words. Thus, in a case of equal billing, the Motor Row District Catalog of Structures lists a Burger King franchise alongside the classic Mitchell Automobile Building and the Golden Pond Restaurant next to the Locomobile headquarters. Including these so-called "non-contributing" entries in the district, it has been suggested, gives city authorities greater control over what the owners can do with the properties in the future.

Chicago landmark status didn't happen easily. "Plans to turn a South Loop area into a landmark district may be in for a bumpy ride," the *Sun-Times* predicted in September 2000. One developer had filed for and possibly even obtained a city permit to demolish the former Ford dealership and erect a six-story condo building with storefronts. Another was seeking permission to raze the one-time Buick outlet next door. Auto and architecture historian Bob Joynt remembers getting an urgent call from fellow historian David Kerr. Somehow, notice of a public hearing by the Commission on Chicago Landmarks had slipped by, and they knew immediately that they had better move quickly to make their case for preservation.

The commission was tasked with making a recommendation to the city council: preserve all, part, or none of the proposed landmark district. Joynt, Kerr, and a third preservation advocate, John O'Halloran, prepared and delivered testimony that attempted to stake out middle ground: allow residential development in the vicinity of Motor Row but repurpose the former dealerships as neighborhood support locations such as pharmacies, dry cleaners, restaurants, and the like. Just when it appeared that Ford, Buick, and perhaps other sites would join the infamous "In Memoriam" list of significant buildings, the ward's effusive alderman, Burton Natarus, had an apparent change of heart and became a preservation supporter.

By long tradition, Chicago aldermen hold life-or-death power over development in their wards. With Natarus's 11th-hour conversion, the landmark district won the approval of the landmarks commission then sailed through the city council. Did someone of considerable influence get involved behind the scenes? Neither Joynt nor Kerr would speculate on the machinations of the Chicago government, but it was no secret that the mayor of Chicago, Richard M. Daley, lived nearby.

There were already 30,000 cars on city streets by 1911, up from only 600 in 1902, ten years after the first horseless carriage appeared. By then, Chicago had earned the distinction of selling more cars than any other city in the country, according to a trade publication of the day, and the unofficial title of the greatest automobile row in the world as well as one of the largest local business groups. Motor Row, however, wasn't preplanned; it evolved in step with this tremendous growth, rolling south on Michigan and onto adjacent Wabash and Indiana Avenues like a mini-boomtown.

Early dealerships were modest, usually two or three stories of conservative design that also housed a garage, repair shop, and offices. These buildings "had quite a bit in common with stables, which were often used as garages and repair shops in the auto's earliest years," according to architectural historian Robert Bruegmann. Later establishments, built after 1910 and south of Sixteenth Street, were much different. They became "elaborate palaces of automobile consumption," in the words of Peter Alter, a curator at the Chicago History Museum. Their architects included some of the city's top individuals and firms—Christian Eckstorm, Alfred Alschuler, Albert Kahn, Holabird & Roche, and Jenney, Mundie & Jensen. Nearly always, the designers relied on white or buff-colored enameled terra-cotta and minimized the use of interior support columns.

The showplaces featured large plate glass windows along the sidewalk so potential buyers on foot or in passing vehicles could get a good look at the models. Before the arrival of the auto dealerships, when Michigan Avenue was upscale residential, 20-foot setbacks were the voluntary norm. But since the first zoning laws weren't enacted until 1923, there was nothing to prevent showroom designers from utilizing every bit of the lot and building right down to the sidewalk, which is exactly what they did. The lots were deep with alleys located at the rear for access to the service departments. Car shoppers entered on Michigan Avenue. Large corner establishments also used side entrances on the east-west streets. Cars stored on upper levels were brought down by ramp or elevator.

All in all, it was a street of dreams that catered to fantasies as well as transportation needs. Salesrooms with alluring exteriors, like the glamorous new movie theaters that were springing up, encouraged passersby to step right in and check out the latest models, imagining themselves behind the steering wheel on the open road, en route to a more enriching life. In the meantime, they could get a preview with a test drive right there on Michigan Avenue.

The prospective customer entered an environment designed to "cast old fogy [sales] methods to the winds," in the words of Motor Age magazine. For instance, a customer entering the Peerless branch at 2500 S. Michigan Avenue (since demolished) passed between a pair of substantial indoor palm trees mounted atop sculpted cement posts, similar to a decorative touch in a hotel lobby. Peerless also offered a more practical feature—an automatic passenger elevator—a rarity for the day. The 1911 magazine article marveled that "in case a salesman desires to take a customer from the first to the fourth floor he simply pushes an electric button which causes the elevator to descend to where he is, the doors being opened simultaneously with the arrival of the car."

The interiors of many of the larger establishments were bathed in another comparatively new concept—indirect lighting—intended to show the display models without any possibility of detracting shadows. Customers waiting to be seen by a salesman could relax in comfortable furniture and perhaps leaf through a brochure or magazine, much as they would at their doctor's office. One dealer removed all salesmen's desks from the main floor except that of the sales manager. Another arranged the desks in a double row through the center of the floor with the models arranged on each side.

Palm trees also greeted the arrival of customers at the Bird-Sykes Company showroom and offices at 2215 S. Michigan Avenue. The trees were just one of the touches that made the building a model for at least 15 that were to follow in 1916 and thereafter, according to Motor Age. Up front was the sales room with one office and a waiting room in the rear. A stairway led to a mezzanine, where the accessory and parts department shared space with offices on either side. The service department took up the rear of the building. Service department windows, like those found on the second floors of other dealerships, were as tall as their counterparts on the first floor in order to maximize natural lighting for the mechanics. Indoor lighting at that time was considered too weak for precision work. Overlooking the ground floor at Bird-Sykes was a balcony accessible by stairway or elevator.

Chicagoans were captivated by this approach to buying a car. The press responded enthusiastically, using adjectives such as "lavish" and "artistic," while the dealers hoped that this blend of style and quality would reinforce the perception of the cars themselves. The public's perception of the higher-end auto buyer—Henry Ford's pitch to the common man notwithstanding—was reinforced by sketch ads of men and women almost always dressed stylishly, even elegantly. Indeed, in the earliest years, automobiles were regarded as playthings of the rich. "Most of them had chauffeurs, and most of them had more than one car," vintage auto collector and authority Herb Lederer points out. A moderately priced car could cost as much as the typical worker earned in a year.

Car shopping was often presented as an activity shared equally by couples. Some ads featured women behind the wheel. A 1919 Pierce-Arrow ad could have been a prototype *New Yorker* cover. The rendering shows a smartly dressed young woman standing beneath a portico, apparently waiting to be picked up by an open-top yellow Pierce-Arrow in the driveway, driven by a man who may or may not be wearing a chauffeur's uniform. The company's early ads were so understated, so intent on selling image, that they didn't mention details about the cars. Even as car prices generally decreased with time, making more models affordable to more people, advertising continued to portray the purchase and ownership of an automobile as the gateway to glamour. "The romance of the automobile," as Lederer describes the experience. "Early cars had a personality."

Other cities developed automobile rows, but Chicago's was almost universally regarded as the most imposing. Car shoppers from across the Midwest descended on this automotive smorgasbord (but they had to bring their own popcorn). Motor Row sales topped $30 million annually by the end of the first decade of the new century. Horses were rarely seen anymore on S. Michigan Avenue.

Prior to the first arrivals on Motor Row, S. Michigan Avenue had evolved from farmland to an affluent residential boulevard. The landscape began to change again after the turn of the century. It's not clear who originated the idea of placing automobiles inside street-level display windows. Maybe the approach was borrowed from department stores like Marshall Field's in Chicago or Hudson's in Detroit. If the concept worked for clothes, shoes, jewelry, and so forth, why not cars?

Initially, many Michigan Avenue residents were reluctant to sell and incur the displeasure of their neighbors who wouldn't welcome the arrival of such an enterprise—unless the money was too good to pass up. After one mansion then another became the future home of an auto merchant, an early form of panic peddling set in. Longtime residents were fearful of encroaching dirt, noise, fumes, auto traffic, oversized showroom windows, and distracting display advertising. Their fears became a self-fulfilling prophecy, and the famed Prairie Avenue residential district immediately east of Michigan Avenue—the bastion of the Fields, Armours, and Pullmans—felt the spillover impact. Time also was catching up with the neighborhood. To some, the grand houses were beginning to seem old-fashioned. The Gold Coast on the Near North Side was becoming the prime locale for the city's wealthiest. The number of mansions in the entire Michigan-Prairie area gradually dwindled to 11.

Time was also catching up with the carriage industry. Bicycle makers, not carriage builders, led the way into the new field of automobile production. The prosperous carriage industry saw no signs of its forthcoming decline much less demise. Early in the development of the auto, "no maker of horse-drawn vehicles did more than stick a tentative toe into the waters of automobile production," according to author John B. Rae of the Massachusetts Institute of Technology (MIT). The Studebaker brothers were no exception. These successful carriage builders wouldn't get into auto manufacturing until later in the game, but their 10-story 1895 building at 625 S. Wabash Avenue attracted the interest of auto dealers. Customers looking for wagons, carriages, or harnesses might also want to check out these new horseless carriages, the auto men reasoned, so they acquired space in surrounding buildings. The Studebakers' Wabash Avenue building, like their earlier location one block east on Michigan Avenue, was the work of Solon S. Beman, fresh from his triumphal creation of George Pullman's factory complex and "model town" 14 miles south of downtown Chicago.

It wasn't until well into the new century that the carriage makers realized that their day was passing and turned to the manufacture of the horseless variety. Makers of both bicycles and carriages left short-term legacies of sorts. Early autos were built to resemble carriages. Wheels sported metal spokes like those of a bike. "Some think of early car builders as tinkerers," says auto historian Herb Lederer, "but they were much more. They were actual engineers."

During the Motor Row era, an astonishing 2,500 makes of automobiles were manufactured in the United States. Practically all the names have passed into history—Locomobile, Roamer, Mitchell, Federal—remembered primarily by vintage car enthusiasts. Their dealerships shared the street with survivors—Ford, Cadillac, Buick, Fiat—along with still others whose names fall somewhere between forgotten and "oh, yeah"—Hudson, Packard, Pierce-Arrow. Automobile Darwinism and the Great Depression took their toll. Some of the dealership buildings survive the manufacturers by nearly a century.

Two of those buildings, the Hudson at 2222 S. Michigan Avenue and the Marmon next door at 2232, became templates for the "grand auto showrooms built during the 1920s," according to the National Register of Historic Places. The agency singles out the "exotic" interior space of the Hudson locale, which incorporated curved woodwork and grand staircases that created "a theatrical setting for selling not only cars but an associated lifestyle." The same could be said of the Marmon dealership.

Designs come and go, just as Motor Row as an automobile sales mecca has come and gone, initially a victim of the Great Depression and later of changing demographics as droves of Chicagoans migrated to the suburbs. Some dealers followed, while others became part of bland stretches of emporiums on city streets to the west such as Ashland, Western, and Cicero Avenues. Sprawling car lots dominated by huge neon signs, flapping pennants, streamers, inflated cartoon characters, and similar gimmicks became substitutes for classic architecture. The original Ford building is now an eye care establishment. Other charter members of Motor Row survive in various guises, a few still sporting their one-time identities in concrete or terra-cotta embedded in their facades, providing visitors with memories bequeathed by a bygone Chicago.

CATALOG OF LANDMARKED STRUCTURES

Catalog No.	Address	Building Name
1	1444 S. Michigan Avenue	Ford Motor Car Company Building
2	1454 S. Michigan Avenue	Buick Motor Company Building
3	1737 S. Michigan Avenue	Maxwell-Briscoe Automobile Company Building
4	1925 S. Michigan Avenue	B.F. Goodrich Company Building
5	2000 S. Michigan Avenue	Locomobile of America Company (No. 1)
6	2200 S. Michigan Avenue	Golden Pond Restaurant
7	2208–2216 S. Michigan Avenue	Bird-Sykes Company Building (No. 1)
8	2218 S. Michigan Avenue	Colonial Trust & Savings Bank
9	2222 S. Michigan Avenue	Hudson Motor Car Company Building
10	2232 S. Michigan Avenue	Marmon Company Building
11	2240–2242 S. Michigan Avenue	Roamer Automobile Company Building
12	2244 S. Michigan Avenue	Building for Seipp Realty Trust
13	2246–2248 S. Michigan Avenue	Centaur Motor Company Building
14	2328 S. Michigan Avenue	Burger King
15	2334–2338 S. Michigan Avenue	Mitchell Automobile Company Building
16	2400–2410 S. Michigan Avenue	Illinois Automobile Club Building
17	2412–2414 S. Michigan Avenue	Cadillac Motor Car Company Building (No. 1)
18	2416 S. Michigan Avenue	Detroit Electric Automobile Company Building

	Address	Building Name
19	2420 S. Michigan Avenue	Pierce-Arrow Auto Company Building
20	2419 S. Michigan Avenue	Building for P.H. Otis
21	2415 S. Michigan Avenue	L&H Buick Sales Company Building
22	2411 S. Michigan Avenue	Speedwell Motor Company Building
23	2401–2409 S. Michigan Avenue	Locomobile Company of America (No. 2)
24	2347–2351 S. Michigan Avenue	Fiat Automobile Company Building (No. 1)
25	2341 S. Michigan Avenue	Cunningham Car Company Building
26	2337 S. Michigan Avenue	Federal Motor Car Company Building
27	2335 S. Michigan Avenue	Unknown Building
28	2333 S. Michigan Avenue	Building for James Walsh
29	2329 S. Michigan Avenue	Premier Auto Car Company Building
30	2325 S. Michigan Avenue	Building for Gerabed Pushman
31	2321–2323 S. Michigan Avenue	Elgin Motor Car Company Building
32	2317–2319 S. Michigan Avenue	Schillo Motor Sales Company Building
33	2313 S. Michigan Avenue	Saxon Automobile Company Building
34	2309–2311 S. Michigan Avenue	Automobile Building for Alfred Cowles
35	2301–2305 S. Michigan Avenue	Cadillac Motor Car Company Building (No. 2)
36	2255 S. Michigan Avenue	Thomas Flyer Garage and Service Building
37	2251–2253 S. Michigan Avenue	Kelly-Springfield Tire Company Building
38	2245 S. Michigan Avenue	Moline Automobile Company Building
39	2239 S. Michigan Avenue	Fiat Automobile Company Building (No. 2)
40	2235 S. Michigan Avenue	Cole Motor Company Building
41	2229 S. Michigan Avenue	Triangle Motors Company Building
42	2221 S. Michigan Avenue	Bird-Sykes Company Building (No. 3)
43	2215 S. Michigan Avenue	Bird-Sykes Company Building (No. 2)
44	2246–2258 S. Indiana Avenue	Rambler Company Building
45	2300–2308 S. Indiana Avenue	Cadillac Motor Car Service Building
46	2312 S. Indiana Avenue	Unknown Building
47	2314–2324 S. Indiana Avenue	Unknown Building
48	2326–2328 S. Indiana Avenue	Cole Automobile Company Building

	Address	Building Name
49	2334 S. Indiana Avenue	J&J Motor Service Inc. Building
50	2338–2342 S. Indiana Avenue	Packard Motor Company Warehouse
51	60 East Twenty-Third Street 2247 S. Wabash Avenue	Oneida Truck Company Building
52	2247 S. Wabash Avenue 60 E. Twenty-Third Street	Oneida Truck Company Building
53	2241–2245 S. Wabash Avenue	Randolph Motor Car Company Building
54	2211–2215 S. Wabash Avenue	Illinois Bell Telephone Company Building
55	43–51 West Cermak Road 2209 S. Wabash Avenue	Chef Luciano's Gourmet Chicken
56	2234 S. Wabash Avenue	Building for Harold A. Howard

MOTOR ROW NORTH OF TWENTY-SECOND STREET. The earliest, most basic, and conventional structures are in this region. (Map by Matthew Owens.)

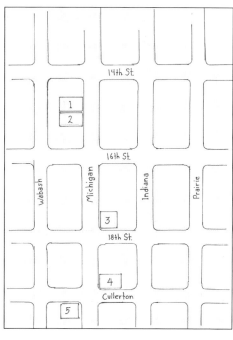

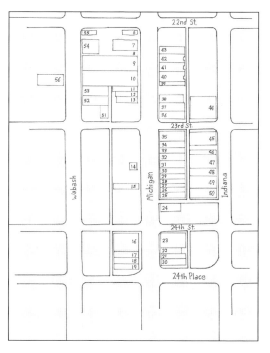

MOTOR ROW SOUTH OF TWENTY-SECOND STREET. As more dealerships were built to the south, the structures became larger and more whimsical, creating a unique architectural environment and a strong sense of place. (Map by Matthew Owens.)

STREET OF DREAMS. Time stands still only a few blocks from the hustle and bustle of Chicago's world-class central business district. A century ago, people crowded these sidewalks shopping for the automobile they felt would change their life. Chicago's Motor Row introduced many to the vehicle that would take them to a better job, possibly help them meet their future spouse, settle in a distant part of the city or suburbs, and provide them with adventure and leisure. Fifty-six landmarked buildings, some remarkably well preserved, offer a fascinating look at architecture and cars during the early age of motoring. (Photograph by John F. Hogan.)

One

STREET OF DREAMS

Chicago's Motor Row was the product of multiple dreams, experienced independently of one another, that converged on the city's near South Side between roughly 1905 and 1936. Visionaries such as Henry Ford, James Packard, and others dreamed of a new way to sell this comparatively new phenomenon called the automobile that was remaking America. To master architects such as Christian Eckstorm, Albert Kahn, and more, the demand for distinctive auto showrooms presented opportunities to dream small and cap their portfolios of more ambitious structures with small jewels. Advertising professionals who trafficked in sizzle as much as steak sold dreams along with the vehicles that would ostensibly fulfill those dreams. Most significantly, American consumers stood ready and eager to buy into the dream of owning their own modern form of transportation that could take them farther, faster to places they would never visit or maybe never heard of. The automobile had become the preeminent symbol of upward mobility, and more than a hundred of them, in every size, price, and style, waited right there on S. Michigan Avenue, inviting buyers to take that first ride.

THEN AND NOW. This photograph and the one on the opposite page, taken more than a century apart, show a section of early Motor Row that doesn't appear to have changed much. The cameras look north from Sixteenth Street, a demarcation line between the smaller, plainer dealerships that comprised the first automotive inhabitants and the larger, flashier buildings that took shape as the row advanced south. The one-time Ford and Buick dealerships are virtually indistinguishable in the upper left. (Courtesy of Chicago History Museum.)

CHICAGO, HOME OF THE SKYSCRAPER. While the development of Chicago's downtown area only a few blocks away saw older buildings replaced with modern commercial and residential high-rises, the value of real estate on S. Michigan Avenue languished, providing little incentive to replace one-time auto dealerships with more modern architecture. Hence, many Motor Row structures have survived multiple spurts of economic growth that doomed other historic buildings farther north. (Photograph by John F. Hogan.)

FROM MANSIONS TO MOTORS. Looking north from Twenty-Seventh Street, about a mile and a half south, provides a view of Michigan Avenue before the advent of Motor Row and later the Stevenson Expressway. Mansions gave way, sometimes grudgingly, to the southward expansion of auto dealerships. (Courtesy of the David Kerr collection.)

STABLES FOR CARS. The earliest auto dealerships were said to have a lot in common with stables that doubled as garages and repair shops. Built in 1892, the Pullman stables at 11201 S. Cottage Grove Avenue accommodated horses owned by the more affluent residents of George Pullman's "model town." Later, the facility became a gas station/repair shop called the Pullman Motor Stables. The now-unoccupied building remains largely unchanged. (Photograph by John F. Hogan.)

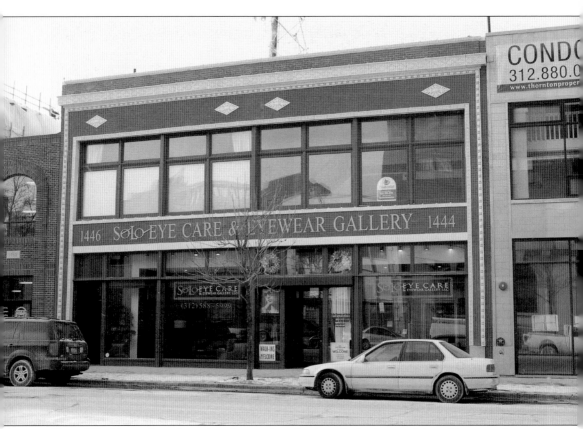

FORD WAS FIRST. It is altogether fitting that the first dealership on Motor Row was designed by the architect who lent his name to the most buildings on Motor Row (12), Christian Albert Eckstorm. Eckstorm's bold, clear lines have endured well at 1444 S. Michigan Avenue, the oldest surviving building on Motor Row. Henry Ford located one of his first dealerships outside Detroit here in 1905, when his company was only in its third year. Business thrived. Before the advent of the assembly line, cars sold faster than the factory could turn them out. Competitors took note, moved nearby, and the development of Motor Row was underway. The Ford team left the two-story building in 1913 for larger quarters a few miles south. The 1444 location is the oldest surviving building on Motor Row and is now occupied by an eye care concern. (Photograph by John S. Maxson.)

MODEL TS AND THEN SOME. This 1910 Model T (photographed in 1946) was typical of the cars that rolled off the Ford assembly line between 1908 and 1927, though each year saw small improvements and style changes. Henry Ford said he was inspired to explore the assembly line process after viewing meatpacking operations at the Chicago Union Stock Yards, specifically the overhead trolley used for dressing beef. The assembly line enabled Ford to slash costs and production time. From the inception of the Model T in 1908 until it ceased production in 1927, 16 million of the cars rolled off the assembly line. (Courtesy of Library of Congress.)

ENTER THE MODEL A. When other manufacturers began attracting Ford's customers with heavier, more reliable, and more powerful cars, Henry Ford reluctantly discontinued the Model T and replaced it with the Model A, which became an overnight sensation. Still a low-priced car, five million Model As were sold during the years 1928–1931 when it was available. Chicago, at the time the country's largest market for automobiles, had a huge impact on what manufacturers would offer, and Model As, like the 1931 Sport Coupe pictured above, were a common sight on the city's streets. (Photograph by John S. Maxson.)

23

UNIVERSAL CHARMER. Henry Ford's Model T continues to be one of the most collectible cars, and several national clubs organize events for enthusiasts around the country and overseas. Many shows feature competition to test the authenticity of the cars and the craftsmanship displayed by restorers. This contemporary picture shows cars waiting to be judged, their brilliantly polished brass headlamps and scrubbed white tires covered with fabric until just before the judges arrive. (Photograph by John S. Maxson.)

BUICK'S ARRIVAL OVERSHADOWED. Christian Eckstorm added the second of his 12 Motor Row buildings in 1907 but eclipsed it the same year with what is arguably his finest achievement, the 15-story International Harvester Company headquarters at 600 S. Michigan Avenue, across from Grant Park. Considered an advanced skyscraper for its time, the structure is now the main building of Columbia College. (Photograph by John F. Hogan.)

BUICK LEAVES ITS MARK. The architect's Buick sales building, two doors south of Ford at 1454 S. Michigan Avenue, continued an impression that Ford and Buick moved in parallel sequence. Both companies were founded in 1903, and from 1907 to 1910, they jockeyed for leadership as the top automaker in the United States. So it was not surprising that Buick followed its competitor two years later and two doors south. Similar in size but less so in appearance, the Buick branch featured curved upper windows and the corporate name imprinted on the stonework. Like its neighbor, it appears in mint condition. In early 2021, the building was vacant. (Photograph by John F. Hogan.)

SEPARATE ROADS. While Ford and Buick seemed to move on parallel roads, there never was any question about marketing strategy. From day one, Buick catered to the higher-end buyer with models such as this 1911 two-cylinder car. Ford provided basic, affordable transportation. (Courtesy of Library of Congress.)

JACK BENNY'S PROP. Comedian Jack Benny got plenty of mileage on his radio and TV shows from jokes about his 1923 Maxwell. The running gag was that Jack was too cheap to buy a newer car. He struggled along with a clunky, unreliable vehicle whose maker had folded in 1925, years before his first program went on the air. In reality, the Maxwell was a serviceable, economical auto and one of the country's top-six sellers until 1920. Designed and built by partners Jonathan Maxwell and Benjamin Briscoe, some models sold for as little as $655. A forerunner of Chrysler, it was the first of the major sellers to use shaft drive instead of chains. (Courtesy of Library of Congress.)

CLASSIC EXAMPLE. Maxwell's former Chicago dealership still dominates the northeast corner of Eighteenth Street and Michigan Avenue (1737 S. Michigan Avenue). It was designed by Ernest Walker in 1909 and is described in the National Register application as "one of the earliest surviving examples of an automobile showroom in Chicago." The four-story, redbrick building is enhanced by buff-colored terra-cotta trim. The stunningly well-restored building is presently owned by the McHugh Construction Co., which maintains its offices there. (Photograph by John F. Hogan.)

TIRE EMPORIUM. The Second Empire (mid-19th-century France) building at 1925 S. Michigan Avenue certainly offered an elegant place to sell something as mundane as automobile tires. Renowned developer Ferdinand Peck lived nearby and supposedly wanted the B.F. Goodrich showroom to blend with the mansions that remained on the avenue. Eckstorm's answer in 1911 was a three-story structure that featured broad display windows on the first two levels and topped them with a mansard roof and three dormers. (Photograph by John F. Hogan.)

IT IS THE THOUGHT THAT COUNTS. The otherwise impressive plaque on the front of the B.F. Goodrich building misspells the architect's last name and substitutes his middle name for his first. Still in top condition, the building is home of the South Asia Institute. (Photograph by John F. Hogan.)

28

NAME ENDURES, CAR DOES NOT. The first Locomobile dealership on the avenue, at 2000 S. Michigan Avenue, also displays the company's name in raised lettering on the building exterior. It was developed in 1909 by John P. Wilson, who built the Ford branch, and designed by the architectural firm Jenney, Mundie & Jensen. The three-story structure featured a particularly high showroom ceiling supported by fluted pillars and a highly polished floor of hardwood mosaics. It was the first building of reinforced concrete in Chicago constructed for the auto sales business. A trade journal of the period described it as "the most imposing and beautiful of all the Chicago branch houses," adding that no auto showroom in New York could compare with it. (Photograph by John F. Hogan.)

STEAM TO GAS. Unlike the 1920 model shown here, the first Locomobile cars were steam-powered. So that no one would miss the point, the company coined the name Locomobile, as in locomotive. However, the name remained after the cars were soon switched to gasoline. During the World War I era, Locomobile was one of the foremost luxury autos in the country and trumpeted the motto "the Best Built Car in America." Pres. Warren G. Harding kept a 1921 model at the White House. (Courtesy of the David Kerr collection.)

A Car for Every Pocketbook. For most of the 39 years the company was in business, Locomobile focused on offering the most precisely engineered and manufactured luxury car on the market. An example is this elegant 1920 Locomobile Model 48 Cape Top Dual Cowl Phaeton owned by Bob and Sheila Joynt. Large in size and heavy in weight, the car offered the passenger the strongest reliability and most comfortable ride that money could buy. Locomobile was headquartered most of its life in Bridgeport, Connecticut. Not a common sight on the streets of Chicago because of its cost, Locomobiles were no longer manufactured after 1929. (Courtesy of the Bob Joynt collection.)

MOBILITY. The Locomobile dealership moved to 2401–2409 S. Michigan Avenue in 1925 and was succeeded by an Auburn Cord outlet in 1931. A nail care shop was doing business on the ground floor in early 2021. In a bow to tradition, the condos above are called the Locomobile Lofts. (Photograph by John F. Hogan.)

OUT OF STEAM. Steam-powered cars were not uncommon in the early 1900s. Locomobile bought the rights to one of its early designs from twin brothers Francis and Freelan Stanley, developers of the legendary Stanley Steamer. Unlike Locomobile, the Stanleys continued to utilize steam. It was a losing bet. As electric starters replaced cranks, fuel efficiency improved, and the cost differential widened, gas models left their steam competition far behind. The Stanley Company went out of business in 1924, but collectors continue to find the simplicity and strong performance of steam-powered cars to be fascinating. This 10-horsepower Model 65 Stanley is owned by Mike and Nancy Roach. (Photograph by John S. Maxson.)

NON-CONTRIBUTOR. The only apparent reason to include this former eatery at 2200 S. Michigan Avenue was to anchor a corner of a map showing a square block packed with contiguous buildings of historical significance. Several other locations fit the same category and are sometimes listed in National Register forms as "non-contributing buildings." Inclusion also restricts future uses of the property. The Golden Pond site is now a dry-cleaning establishment. (Photograph by John F. Hogan.)

BIRD-SYKES SOLD MULTIPLE BRANDS. Noted architect Christian Eckstorm began his career in Chicago with the firm Cobb & Frost, later managing the office for Henry Ives Cobb. Eckstorm designed the Byrd-Sykes Company dealership at 2208–2216 S. Michigan Avenue in 1910, incorporating the signature large street-level windows into his plan. (Photograph by John F. Hogan.)

FOLLOW THE MONEY. The inclusion of the former Colonial Bank building serves the same purpose as the former Golden Pond site. It maintains the unbroken succession of addresses on the west side of Michigan Avenue between Twenty-Second and Twenty-Third Streets but at the same time retains a somewhat tenuous connection to the auto business. "The Colonial was the dealers' bank," says historian Bob Joynt. "They borrowed money there." The small building at 2218 S. Michigan Avenue was constructed in 1919 and remains virtually unchanged except for wear and tear, a condition protected by a facade that was only recently removed. It remains vacant. (Photograph by John F. Hogan.)

CROWNING ACHIEVEMENTS. Architect Alfred Alschuler contributed a pair of crown jewels to Motor Row in 1922—the Hudson and Marmon buildings at 2222 and 2232 S. Michigan Avenue. Each occupied the deepest lots in the district, extending one full block from Michigan Avenue to Wabash Avenue on the west. (Photograph by John F. Hogan.)

WHITE TERRA-COTTA PALACE. The three-story Hudson showroom at 2222 S. Michigan Avenue was described as a white terra-cotta palace in the Spanish baroque style and compared to the glamorous new movie theaters. Like the theaters, the interior contained carved woodwork and grand staircases. Four large plate glass windows—two on each side of an arched entranceway—alternately showcased Hudsons and the company's lower-end model, the Essex. Much of the building's majestic exterior was covered by a tarp in early 2021 in anticipation of renovation. (Courtesy of the David Kerr collection.)

HUDSON'S SUPER START. Hudson found immediate success in the marketplace after its introduction in 1909. Detroit department store magnate Joseph L. Hudson contributed his name along with substantial capital and help from eight other businessmen to introduce a car that would be competitive in the lower-priced field. In 1910, the company's first full year of operation, the Hudson Twenty sold more than 4,500 units, the best initial year of any car in the young industry. The 1920 Hudson Super Six is seen here in Washington, DC, with government buildings in the background. The company enjoyed one of the longer runs among the now-defunct makes represented on Motor Row, from 1909 to 1954. The latter year saw Hudson merge with Nash-Kelvinator to form American Motors Corporation (AMC). The Hudson name was dropped in 1957. (Courtesy of Library of Congress.)

DYNAMIC DUO. Though less ornate and one story shorter than its next-door neighbor, Hudson, the Marmon dealership at 2232 S. Michigan Avenue incorporated some of the same features, including four plate glass display windows separated by an arched entranceway. The company name appears boldly at the top of the arch as well as less conspicuously at the peak of the building. (Photograph by John S. Maxson.)

BEHIND THE DOORS . . . The restored entry to the Marmon showroom brings back the grandeur of this magnificent auto palace. (Photograph by John F. Hogan.)

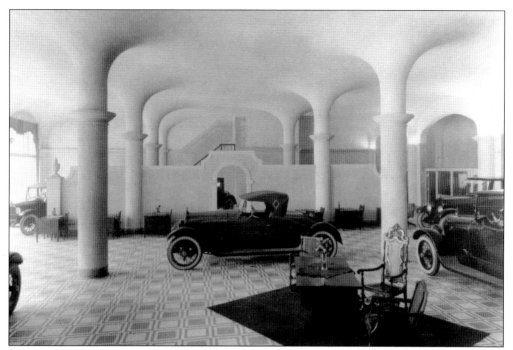

SOMETHING TO BEHOLD. The interior of the Marmon showroom was something to behold with its "tall ceilings and supporting columns that arch out at the top and flow into the ceiling," in the words of historian David Kerr's thesis. "Coupled with room dividers that had arched openings and an ornate staircase and decorated with plants and Persian carpets, a visitor might expect to run into the Sheik of Araby." (Courtesy of the David Kerr collection.)

Interior of the new Maxwell home in Chicago. These are the quarters previously housing Harry Newman, Inc.

MAXWELLS ON DISPLAY. The Marmon showroom compares favorably to the interior of the more spartan Maxwell showroom down the street at 1737 S. Michigan Avenue. (Courtesy of the David Kerr collection.)

ARCHITECTURAL INTEGRITY.
This vintage photograph
of the Marmon Building
illustrates the originality of
the structure. It is common
to see other Motor Row
buildings repurposed by
bricking up windows and
deleting architectural
ornamentation. Though a
century old, the Marmon
Building has not suffered
this modernization.
(Courtesy of the David
Kerr collection.)

RECORD OF ACHIEVEMENTS. Indianapolis-based Marmon Motor Car Company logged several
signal achievements before going under in 1933. A Marmon race car, the Marmon Wasp, driven
by company engineer Ray Harroun, won the first Indy 500 in 1911. Marmon introduced the first
rearview mirror, the short-lived V-16 engine, and the use of aluminum in auto manufacturing. An
industry that sold lifestyle along with transportation could not have found a better standard bearer
for the carefree 1920s than that high priest of the Jazz Age, celebrated author F. Scott Fitzgerald,
who proudly drove a Marmon. (Courtesy of the John S. Maxson collection.)

Not Bad for a Neighborhood Kid. The Marmon building's—and Hudson's—designer, Alfred S. Alschuler, was Chicago-born and the product of the city's public school system. He obtained a master of science degree from Armour Institute of Technology (now Illinois Institute of Technology—IIT) and worked for Dankmar Adler of Adler and Sullivan fame before embarking on his own. Perhaps his most famous work still standing is the London Guaranty Building (now the London House) at the southwest corner of Michigan Avenue and Wacker Drive (1922–1923). (Photograph by John F. Hogan.)

What Next for Marmon Site? Not long before his death in March 2021, legendary investor, philanthropist, and antique car collector Richard Driehaus purchased the Marmon Building and installed 25 to 30 of his 72-car collection inside, away from public view. The Driehaus collection is regarded by vintage car enthusiasts as one of the premier assemblages in the Midwest. It is believed that Driehaus had planned to develop the Marmon Building into an event center for use by charitable organizations using the vintage cars as background in a former showroom said to remain in excellent condition. The rest of the collection is housed at a location southwest of downtown. Driehaus's heirs have not indicated their plans for the Marmon site, but a replication of its glory days of the 1920s would be greeted with cheers from the vintage auto and architecture communities. (Photograph by John S. Maxson.)

NOT BRED FOR THE LONG RUN. Named for a racehorse and marketed as "America's Smartest Car," the stylish Roamer began life on Motor Row the year of its inception in Upstate New York, 1916. It was the flagship of the Barley Motor Car Co., which soon moved production to Kalamazoo, Michigan. Roamers were big cars, seating four to seven with engines up to 75 horsepower. Its nickel-plated grill was modeled after that of Rolls-Royce. The Barley Company could not blame the Depression for its demise. It went out of business in 1929, before the stock market crash. Roamer's two-story headquarters at 2440–2442 S. Michigan Avenue was another of Eckstorm's small masterpieces. A hair salon was located there in 2021. Other sections of the building were for rent while the entire structure was for sale. (Photograph by John F. Hogan.)

No Takers. Developer Edwin Seipp erected this building at 2244 S. Michigan Avenue in 1917, at the same time he built the Moline Auto sales emporium across the street. According to National Register data, Seipp was unsuccessful in finding a tenant. In 2021, the space was occupied by Bar 22. (Photograph by John F. Hogan.)

IN IT FOR THE SHORT HAUL. The Centaur Motor Vehicle Company of Buffalo, New York, had the shortest manufacturing life of any firm represented on Motor Row. In fact, Centaur stopped making cars a year before Motor Row was born. Centaur sold only a small number of electric and gasoline-powered cars between 1902 and 1904 but continued in business as a dealer offering Cadillacs, Yales, and Abbott-Detroits. Centaur entered the Chicago marketplace in 1912, setting up shop in a building at 2246–2248 S. Michigan Avenue designed by architect E.J. Ornstein. It is not known how long the company remained in business. Its building was vacant and for sale in 2021. (Photograph by John F. Hogan.)

HOLD THE LETTUCE. The address listed in the Motor Row Catalog, 2224 S. Michigan Avenue, would place Burger King in the middle of space occupied since 1922 by the Hudson building. The existing Burger King is in the next block south, at 2328, and is correctly identified in other listings. That restaurant is flanked by its parking lot on the north and the Mitchell Automobile building on the south. According to published reports, the Burger King franchise lease was due to expire in 2021, and the restaurant, parking lot, and surrounding space were purchased by a real estate venture in February 2020 for $6.3 million. The new owners reportedly planned to build a boutique hotel on the site, but the continuing COVID-19 pandemic put those intentions on hold. (Photograph by John F. Hogan.)

THE LITTLE CAR THAT COULD. A 1911 auto trade publication states that 2328 S. Michigan Avenue was "the Chicago home of the Brush runabout." The Brush was a little car that could, a single-cylinder machine promoted as "Everyman's Car" that sold for as little as $350. In 1908, a couple named Trinkle drove their Brush Runabout to the top of Pike's Peak, a feat that only two other autos had accomplished. The ascent was part of the Trinkles' 2,300-mile drive across America. The Brush Runabout, like the 1910 model pictured, incorporated a number of unique features that included wooden frames, axles, and wheels. The Highland Park, Michigan, company lasted only from 1907 to 1913 under the leadership of a man with arguably the most patrician-sounding name of all automakers, Alanson Partridge Brush. His company's demise was part of a general decline in the popularity of runabouts because of a lack of protection against the weather. (Courtesy of John S. Maxson.)

BRUSHES AND HENRYS. Brush autos also were sold from a charming three-story building at 1507 S. Michigan Avenue that survives in mint condition but did not qualify for inclusion on the list of the "Fortunate Fifty-Six." Brush shared space in the showroom with the Henry, a car built by the Henry Motor Car Company of Muskegon, Michigan. The Henry was a big, expensive car—a five-seater with engines of 20, 35, and 40 horsepower. Models featuring the 35-horsepower engine sold for $1,750. The Henry enjoyed an even shorter lifespan than its stablemate, from 1910 to 1912. (Photograph by John F. Hogan.)

BIG CARS, BIG BUILDING. The Mitchell Automobile Company building at 2334–2338 S. Michigan Avenue reflected the look of the cars themselves—large and fashionable. At four stories and a half-block deep, the Mitchell Building, designed by Jarvis Hunt, is one of only two on the west side of the 2300 block of S. Michigan Avenue. The other is the Burger King outlet. (Photograph by John F. Hogan.)

M IS FOR MITCHELL. A bold white-on-blue "M" monogram still dominates the top and center of the Mitchell Building. In early 2021, the property was for sale and undergoing exterior repairs. (Photograph by John F. Hogan.)

TWENTY-YEAR STREAK. Mitchell offered touring cars of four, six, and eight cylinders, including this F-50 White Streak. Unlike its handsome Chicago building, which projects durability, the company lasted only from 1903 to 1923. (Courtesy of Library of Congress.)

TIME STANDS STILL. The time is always 2:50 according to the clock above the former Illinois Automobile Club building at 2400 S. Michigan Avenue. As far as anyone knows, the frozen hands hold no special meaning, like, say, the hands of the Ferry Building clock in San Francisco that stopped and remained that way for some time after the earthquakes of 1906 and 1989. Maybe, when the time is appropriate, the Auto Club clock will run again to signal the full restoration of Motor Row's glory. In the meantime, the building remains the youngest and most distinctive of the 56 entries in the register of noteworthy sites. (Photograph by John S. Maxson.)

ENDING WITH A FLOURISH. As noted, Motor Row's development began in earnest in 1905 with the construction of Ford's modest two-story showroom at Fourteenth Street and Michigan Avenue. It ended with a flourish, 31 years later and 10 blocks south, with the construction of the Illinois Automotive Club headquarters, designed by renowned Chicago architect Philip Brooks Maher, who was also responsible for the Gary, Indiana, city hall and the Woman's Athletic Club building at 625 N. Michigan Avenue. The two Motor Row structures offer a microcosm of the district's evolution from modest to lavish. (Photograph by John S. Maxson.)

IT MUST HAVE BEEN SWELL. The three-story Auto Club at 2400 S. Michigan Avenue never sold cars or anything else except a promise to members to deliver a 21-story facility with a dance floor, gym, swimming pool, and other amenities. The Depression shattered that grandiose dream, but even the scaled-back version capped the row with panache and gave auto enthusiasts, including many dealers, a first-rate place to gather with kindred spirits. (Photograph by John S. Maxson.)

EVEN THE WEATHERVANE HAD AN AUTO THEME. The club was operated by a manager who was provided with his own living quarters on-site. It supplanted one of the city's leading Jewish clubs, the Standard, which razed its building and moved downtown. Built to resemble a Spanish mission, the beige Auto Club is topped by the three-story clock tower, complete with a weathervane in the form of a car. (Photograph by John S. Maxson.)

SEEKING KIM NOVAK. A fan of classic movies might envision Jimmy Stewart tailing Kim Novak in the San Francisco Mission District scene from *Vertigo*. The *Chicago Defender*, the city's leading African American newspaper, took over the premises in 1958 and moved its presses into the swimming pool. The paper relocated in 2005. The building is currently home to Revel Motor Row, which rents space for meetings and social events. (Photograph by John S. Maxson.)

FORD VS. CADILLAC. A dispute between Henry Ford and some of his initial investors in 1902 led to the formation of two of the most iconic auto dynasties in history. Ford and several key partners left the company named for himself, dropped the automaker's first name from the corporate title, and organized the Ford Motor Company in 1903. The financial backers he left behind brought in an engineering whiz who repurposed the original company's manufacturing facilities, renamed the firm in honor of the French explorer who founded Detroit, and by the end of 1902, were turning out the first Cadillacs. The two original models were 10-horsepower, two-seater horseless carriages, a modest start that ultimately led to the well-deserved accolade "Standard of the World." (Courtesy of Library of Congress.)

LEAVING THEM IN THE DUST. Cadillac introduced numerous technological advances that included precision engineering, the introduction of the first fully enclosed car by a "volume manufacturer," and the first car to incorporate electrical starting, ignition, and lighting. The 1915 V-8 could routinely reach speeds of 65 miles per hour, faster than most roads could safely accommodate. The car pictured here is a 1914 Cadillac once owned by Bob Lederer. (Photograph by John S. Maxson.)

MODEST BEGINNING. Cadillac's first entry on Motor Row was constructed in 1909, the year it became part of General Motors as its top-of-the-line purveyor of large luxury vehicles. The modest two-story building at 2412–2414 S. Michigan Avenue hardly reflected the image of the brand. Designed by Mundie & Jensen, it incorporated the large ground-floor display windows that were the norm and smaller upper windows framed by buff-colored terra-cotta. Two years later, Cadillac opened a second, much more impressive showroom at 2301–2305 S. Michigan Avenue. The architect was Holabird & Roche. The first location was for lease at the end of 2020. (Photograph by John F. Hogan.)

CLARA FORD'S CHOICE. Here is a trick question: which make of car was driven by Clara Ford, Henry's wife? The answer is a Detroit Electric. Clara was so pleased with her 1914 model that she continued to drive it well into the 1930s. Women drivers who disdained the need to crank-start an internal combustion engine and doctors who relied on a quick, reliable start to respond to an emergency were drawn to electric vehicles typified by the Detroit Electric. The cars were powered by a rechargeable lead-acid battery that could operate for about 80 miles between charges. The need for frequent charges and top speeds of only about 20 miles an hour mostly, but not always (note the photograph), limited usage to urban driving. Built by the Detroit Electric Car Company, the square-bodied vehicles reached peak popularity in the 1910s with sales of 1,000 to 2,000 a year nationally. (Courtesy of the William Tyre collection.)

GASLESS CARRIAGE. Detroit Electric was one of the earlier arrivals on Motor Row, occupying space at 2416 S. Michigan Avenue, designed by Mundie & Jensen for developer Bryan Lathrop in 1909. The two-story, buff-colored building provided display viewing on each side of the entrance with five double windows fronting the second floor. (Photograph by John F. Hogan.)

MANAGING THE IMAGE OF ELECTRIC CARS. As pointed out previously, the early era of motoring saw the popularity of electric vehicles strengthened by the fact that the car moved with the push of a button. But the range and reliability of electric vehicles had to be proven. Perhaps as a publicity stunt, this Detroit Electric was driven to the top of Pike's Peak, the 14,000-foot summit near Colorado Springs, Colorado, a steep climb many gasoline cars of the day could not achieve. (Courtesy of Library of Congress.)

THE WOMEN CHECK IN. Bryan Lathrop and his sister, Florence Lathrop Page, were atypical of early Motor Row developers. Building auto showrooms represented a departure for these Chicago society figures. Born into a distinguished Virginia family, the Lathrops developed five Motor Row buildings, all but one credited to Bryan. They were Cadillac No. 1 (1909), shown above at 2412 S. Michigan Avenue, Detroit Electric (1909), Fiat No. 1 (1910), and Mitchell (1910). The Premier building (1909) carries the imprint of Florence, one of three women recognized as Motor Row developers. (Photograph by John F. Hogan.)

A MAN FOR ALL SEASONS. By the time he became involved with auto showrooms late in life (his mid-60s), Byron Lathrop was already a wealthy man many times over from real estate and life insurance ventures. He was an art collector, longtime president of the Chicago Symphony Orchestra and Graceland Cemetery, and trustee of the Newberry Library and Art Institute of Chicago. His house at 120 E. Bellevue Place is a Chicago landmark. (Photograph by John F. Hogan.)

CARS TO KIDS. Children now gather where car salesmen once reigned. The 2416 S. Michigan Avenue building, once the Detroit Electric automobile showroom, is presently the site of a privately operated preschool. (Photograph by John F. Hogan.)

ELECTRIC COMPETITORS. A Detroit Electric competitor, the Borland-Grannis Company, was another whose Chicago showroom at 2634 S. Michigan Avenue did not survive the construction of the Stevenson Expressway. The Borland Electric coupe was a rather boxy-looking five-passenger model that resembled a fancy enclosed carriage. (Courtesy of Library of Congress.)

THE YEARS HAVE NOT BEEN KIND. Just before the Stevenson Expressway abruptly ends the southward expanse of Motor Row stands a drab building that does not reflect the luxury cars that once called it home. Where two display windows used to face the sidewalk outside 2420 S. Michigan Avenue, the space has been covered over. This two-story building was the Paulman & Co. dealership, identified in later years as the Pierce-Arrow Company building. It was designed in 1909 by Mundie & Jensen. In the words of a trade publication of the day, Paulman & Co. "does an exclusive business with the wealthiest section of Chicago's populace." Its one-time Chicago showroom is occupied by an advertising agency. (Photograph by John F. Hogan.)

LIGHTING THE WAY. Pierce-Arrow automobiles could be identified by the headlights, which stylistically were a part of the front fenders long before this became the standard for all cars. (Photograph by John S. Maxson.)

AUTO OF PRESIDENTS. The outsize Pierce-Arrow was the ultimate in luxury, a status symbol owned by tycoons, Hollywood celebrities, and US presidents. Pres. William Howard Taft (who needed ample seating space) ordered two and made them the first official White House cars. Outgoing president Woodrow Wilson and his successor, Warren Harding, rode in an open-bodied Pierce-Arrow to the latter's inauguration in 1921. The Buffalo, New York, company went out of business in 1938. (Courtesy of the David Kerr collection.)

"IF YOU BUILD IT, THEY WILL COME." Or maybe not. At least three buildings on Motor Row were erected by developers who apparently anticipated leasing or selling them, the way John P. Wilson got the Street of Dreams started when he handed the keys to 1444 to Henry Ford, so to speak. If any of the three ever functioned as auto showrooms, they are not identified as such in the Motor Row District Catalog of Structures or accompanying documents. Ironically, all three were designed by Christian Eckstorm. They are the P.H. Otis Building at 2419 S. Michigan Avenue (1915). It is currently occupied by one of the few auto-related operations on the row, an automotive warehouse distributor. Also, there is the James Walsh Building, 2333 S. Michigan Avenue (1916). The site remains vacant. It is followed by the Gerabed Pushman Building, 2325 S. Michigan Avenue (1912), where the ground floor has been vacant. (Photograph by John F. Hogan.)

INDEPENDENT'S DAY. Nine years after Eckstorm designed the second building on Motor Row, the Buick Company dealership next door to Ford at 1454 S. Michigan Avenue, he did one for an independent Buick dealer. This was the L&H Buick Sales Company building at the opposite end of the row, 2415 S. Michigan Avenue. L&H Sales (1916) was a throwback to the earlier, smaller outlets at a time when the palatial dealerships were about to emerge. Flanked by doorways, the display window was large enough for only one model. A women's clinic is the current occupant. (Photograph by John F. Hogan.)

SHORT RUN. Bad luck dogged the short, unhappy life of the Speedwell Motor Car Company of Dayton, Ohio. Founded in 1907, the company lasted only until 1914. It never recovered from a devastating flood in 1913 that severely damaged its factory and inventory. A 1910 newspaper ad was aimed at car owners who had paid $3,500 or $4,000 for their vehicles, suggesting that a Speedwell could deliver comparable quality "in any kind of body you desire" for $2,500. The following year, the company rolled out a two-door model it called a sedan, presumably the first recorded use of the term for an automobile. What once were the display windows of the C.E. and R.W. Beach–designed building at 2411 S. Michigan Avenue (1909) have been replaced by brickwork, leaving only a doorway. The space was occupied by a banquet hall and meeting facility in 2021. (Photograph by John F. Hogan.)

Two

THE JOURNEY BEGINS HERE

Bookended by the oldest and newest of the 56 sites, Motor Row lives on 28 acres of urban landscape waiting to be explored. The last of the dealerships, a Fiat–Alfa Romeo outlet, departed in 2009 from the one-time Auburn-Cord location. A surprising number of the classic buildings have survived, the legacy of some of the nation's foremost architects. Taken in total, Motor Row does not overwhelm. The survivors standing between Ford and the Illinois Automobile Club have to be examined individually to be fully appreciated. There are subtleties that need to be probed, like those of a Monet or Renoir—the raised lettering on the Locomobile or Buick buildings, the blends of terra-cotta and glass, the use of pastels, and the arched entranceways. Motor Row is cuisine meant to be savored one bite at a time.

ENDING ON A HIGH NOTE. Locomobile's exit from its second, larger space at 2401–2409 S. Michigan Avenue opened the way for a late Motor Row arrival that arguably gained more prestige among auto aficionados after its demise than before. The Auburn Automobile Company of Auburn, Indiana, took over the location in 1931, two years after Locomobile stopped making cars. Auburns and Cords were sold there until 1936, the year before it ceased production. Auburn's departure foreshadowed the end of the Motor Row era itself. (Photograph by John F. Hogan.)

ERRAT LOBBAN CORD ARRIVES. The auto world had not seen anything quite like it. Aggressive styling and advanced engineering were hallmarks of the Auburn Company, which traced its roots to an early-20th-century carriage maker. Following a switch to automobiles and ownership changes, the company emerged in the mid-1920s under the imaginative leadership of Errat Lobban Cord, who added a sleekly styled, quite expensive car to the more moderately priced Auburn lineup and named it for himself. (On the subject of names, Cord strongly disliked his first two and called himself "E.L.") (Courtesy of the John S. Maxson collection.)

AIRPLANES TOO. E.L. Cord's corporate empire included many endeavors, including airplane manufacturing. From 1929 to 1934, he headed the Stinson Aircraft Company of Dayton, Ohio. Cord did not sell planes at his auto dealerships. This inclusion apparently was done as a promotion. (Courtesy of the David Kerr collection.)

STYLISH FEATURES. Features of the Auburn were sporty, aggressive styling, jackrabbit performance (a supercharged model was available), and a reputation for being fun to drive. Too expensive for Depression-era consumers, the company declared bankruptcy and, in 1940, was reorganized into the Auburn Central Manufacturing Corporation (ACM), which built car bodies. Over 150,000 Jeep bodies were shipped by ACM to Willys-Overland and Ford, the companies with government contracts to build the small military vehicles. After World War II, ACM went from building automobile components to manufacturing kitchen sinks, appliances, and cabinets. (Courtesy of the David Kurtz collection.)

INNOVATION, ENGINEERING, AND STYLING. The Cord was the first American production vehicle to use front-wheel drive. By placing the flywheel and transmission at the front of the engine, road clearance at the rear axle was no longer an issue, and the car could be designed to be much lower. Also, with the entire drivetrain under the hood, there was no hump in the front or rear passengers' compartment, making the car much roomier. As much a sensation today as they were when first introduced in 1929, Cord cars like the one pictured here draw crowds at shows and parades. (Courtesy of the David Kurtz collection.)

THE INDIANA ROLLS. In 1926, Auburn entered a partnership with the Duesenberg Corporation and produced a line of even higher-priced luxury vehicles. "It was simply one of the greatest cars ever built," in the opinion of historian Bob Joynt. In essence, the Duesenberg became Indiana's answer to the Rolls-Royce. But after the stock market crashed in late 1929, a manufacturer of upscale vehicles faced a precarious future. Duesenberg went out of business in 1937. (Courtesy of the David Kurtz collection.)

BEAUTIFUL LEGACY. The Auburn Company went under in 1937 but left a marvelous legacy, its spacious three-story art deco headquarters in Auburn, Indiana, now the home of the Auburn Cord Duesenberg Automobile Museum. The museum joined Motor Row as a National Historic Landmark in 2005. An investment management firm does business at Auburn's former Chicago location. (Courtesy of the David Kurtz collection.)

TRAGIC LEGACY. The prestigious Chicago architecture firm Holabird & Roche delivered one of its six additions to Motor Row with the unveiling of the first of two Fiat showrooms in 1910. Fiat No. 1, at 2347 S. Michigan Avenue, presented a "strikingly modern appearance" for a structure that old, in the view of a present-day critic. The two-story building's facade is almost entirely constructed of plate-glass display windows while its roof slopes gently away from the street. After Fiat left the building, it became occupied by the Stevens-Duryea Company, manufacturer of exclusive cars, until 1927. Tragedy struck the property in February 2003 when the ground floor was occupied by the Epitome Chicago restaurant and the upper level was home of the E2 nightclub. The club was packed when a brawl occurred, and security guards responded with pepper spray. Panicked by the commotion and chemical odor, patrons rushed for the only exit and found the doors closed to prevent the return of the instigators. Twenty-one people died, and more than 50 were injured in a mass pileup that accompanied the stampede. The club was operating in spite of 11 building code violations, including overcrowding. Its two owners were each sentenced to two-year prison terms. Epitome and E2 never reopened. The building's modern restaurant/nightclub facade was removed to restore the exterior to its original appearance, but the site remained closed by city order in 2021 and was for sale or lease. (Photograph by John F. Hogan.)

ADMIRABLE TRACK RECORD. William Holabird and Martin Roche were well established before they turned to automobile showroom design. A particularly fruitful year was 1895, when the partners completed work on Fort Sheridan, the Army installation north of the city on Lake Michigan, and the classic Marquette Building, which still stands on the northwest corner of Dearborn and Adams Streets. In the mid-1920s, Holabird & Roche designed the third iteration of the Palmer House hotel at State and Monroe Streets. (Photograph by John F. Hogan.)

FOREIGN ARRIVAL. Italian automaker Fiat began exporting cars to the United States in 1908 then built its first US factory in 1910 in Upstate New York. Fiats did not come cheap. They rose from an initial average of $4,000 to $6,400 in 1918. By comparison, Model T Fords sold for $825 in 1908 and, thanks to the company's economies of scale, dropped to $525 by 1918. (Courtesy of the John S. Maxson collection.)

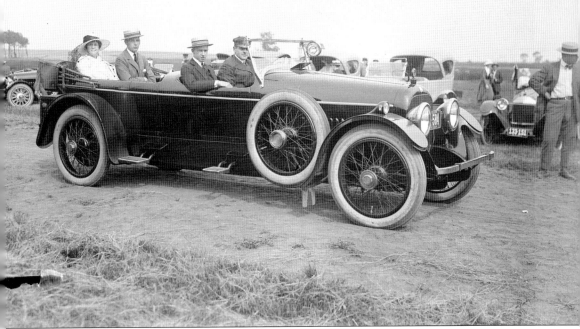

MRS. JAS. KIDDER

JAY LENO OWNS ONE. Size, quality, and high prices were hallmarks of the cars like this 1917 model that were produced by James Cunningham, Son and Company of Rochester, New York, from 1908 to 1931. The Cunningham represented the antithesis of Henry Ford and his production line. Not only were Cunningham autos hand-built, the company added a do-it-yourself touch by inviting purchasers to commission their own bodywork and assisted them with design and execution. This option could easily double the price of cars that already sold at an average of $3,500 to $5,500. A limousine topped out at $8,100. Since the cars were built by hand, production was limited. Four hundred fifty workers turned out an average of fewer than 700 vehicles a year. The Cunningham might be gone but has not been totally forgotten. In 2012, TV's Jay Leno showed off his 1920 Cunningham roadster on his program *Jay Leno's Garage*. (Courtesy of the John S. Maxson collection.)

STILL LOOKING GOOD. Cunningham's Chicago quarters at 2341 S. Michigan Avenue have survived the years in top shape. One of the largest of the early Motor Row buildings (1910), the four-story structure's top three levels feature abundant window space trimmed in striking blue. The street-level display windows, however, have been replaced by opaque construction materials. Possibly reflecting its hands-on style of manufacturing, the Cunningham Company worked directly with architect F.E. Davidson in perfecting the details of its Chicago home. The building now contains lofts and event space. (Photograph by John F. Hogan.)

HANDOUTS. Dealers used a variety of enticements to woo customers such as movies, literature, and various handouts. Cunningham offered this attractive paperweight. (Courtesy of the David Kerr collection.)

An Ideal Car for
Business and Professional Men

The
FEDERAL

Model C Runabout, $600

A car for every day service, constructed upon the simplest lines to attain the maximum of power, speed and
durability, and needs no mechanical
knowledge to operate it successfully

It is a car of style and practicability

If you are contemplating the purchase of
a car, this is the car for you to buy

Dealers, this is the car for you to handle
Write for full particulars

Federal Automobile Co.
40th St. and Wentworth Ave., Chicago, Ill.

BUSINESSMEN'S SPECIAL. Chicago-based Federal Motor Car Co. manufactured either "a very crude looking runabout," in the words of a modern-day publication, or "An Ideal Car for Business and Professional Men," according to a 1907 company ad. Both views probably were correct at the time they were expressed. The two-cylinder, 12-horsepower 1907 Federal was "a car for everyday service . . . and needs no mechanical knowledge to operate it," the company proclaimed. It was indeed a simple-looking machine that sold for $600, a price easily affordable, one would think, by the two extremely well-dressed "business or professional" men rendered in the ad. (Courtesy of the William Tyre collection.)

CARS TO COCKTAILS. The Federal was sold from a three-story building at 2339 S. Michigan Avenue, designed in 1910 by architect David Robertson. In early 2021, the Motor Row Brewery microbrewery and pub was succeeded by the more upscale Bassline Bar and Lounge, which specializes in private events. (Photograph by John F. Hogan.)

MOTOR ROW MYSTERY. The equally attractive building at 2335 S. Michigan Avenue, next door to the one-time Federal outlet, is a Motor Row mystery. National Register information reveals only that the three-story structure was also built around 1910, architect, developer, occupant, and other details unknown. Nonetheless, the mystery building fits nicely with its neighbors. A cosmetic medical spa was the ground floor tenant in late 2020. (Photograph by John F. Hogan.)

HARD TO MISS. Developer Florence Lathrop Page had to be pleased with Holabird & Roche's familiar clean, classic treatment that marks the Premier Auto Car Company building at 2329 S. Michigan Avenue. There is no mistaking the name of the car that was sold here; the word Premier appears above each of the three stories. A pediatrics office occupies the ground level. The upper stories were for lease. (Photograph by John F. Hogan.)

MORE PREMIER VICTORIES

At Chicago, July 3d and 4th The
PREMIER
"The Quality Car"
Air Cooled

again demonstrated its ability to run fast—to do good work on the track as well as on the road—by defeating the fastest cars in the great free-for-all Hawthorne Handicap Race and the free-for-all Corrigan Sweepstakes—and winning the Silver Cups for these events, the only two in which it competed.

The car accomplishing this feat was the Premier racing car—the largest and most powerful four-cylinder, air-cooled car ever built.

This car is a reproduction, in all essential details of construction, of our regular stock Model L De Luxe car, herewith illustrated. No cars upon the market today have demonstrated their worth for general use so fully as the Premier—comfortable, stylish, fast, strong, enduring, simple, economical, strong irreversible steering gear, large section tires, detachable tonneau—all the elements necessary or desirable for a highly satisfactory car.

See our nearest agent or send for catalogue (R).

SPECIFICATIONS

Pressed steel frame, 4¼x4¼ in. vertical motor, 20-24 M.P., three speeds forward and reverse, selective type sliding gear transmission, 106 in. wheel base, 32 in. wheels, 4 in. G. & J. Clincher tires, very strong I-beam section front axle, full elliptic springs with Premier shock-absorbing head; gasoline tank, 12 gallons capacity; upholstered in best hand-buffed, water grained leather, hair padded; detachable tonneau. Body and gear, Brewster Green or Carmine, with equipment of two handsome head-lights, two oil side lamps, oil tonneau lamp, generator, tube horn and full kits of tire and repair tools.

Model L, De Luxe Car

Premier Motor Mfg. Company

Indianapolis, Ind., U. S. A.

Members American Motor Car Mfrs. Ass'n.

CHECK OUT THE UPHOLSTERY. The first Premier in 1904 was a 40-horsepower touring car that seated six and cost $5,000. Two models that debuted in 1906 (Model L, shown in the ad, and Model F) carried price tags of $1,250 to $2,250. Unlike many other automakers, Premier played up the use of "luxurious upholstering." Later, the Indianapolis-based company introduced a sporty two-seat roadster. The short-lived Badger Motor Car Company of Columbus, Wisconsin, sold cars from the Premier building. Four-cylinder Badgers were marketed as high-powered, high-quality cars that could be found in the medium-price range. Founded in 1910, the company was gone a year later. Its principals were a local clothier, banker, and grocer. Only 237 Badgers were produced before bankruptcy intervened. (Courtesy of the William Tyre collection.)

HOIST SAIL. In the midst of a district dedicated to the automobile, a maritime-related company occupies a niche. The operation behind the bright facade at 2321–2323 S. Michigan Avenue is UK Sailmakers, which both manufactures and repairs sails. Originally, the two-story building with the oversized second floor was the home of the Elgin Motor Car Company, designed by architect L.M. Mitchell in 1920. (Photograph by John F. Hogan.)

CARS BUILT TO ENDURE, NOT COMPANY. Bearing the name of one city west of Chicago but built in another (Argo), the first Elgins appeared in 1916. Production was moved to Indianapolis in 1923, where it remained until the company folded two years later. Elgin specialized in five-passenger touring cars and four-passenger roadsters. The company promised endurance and economy. A 1917 six-cylinder touring car was priced at $985. (Courtesy of the William Tyre collection.)

DEALER OFFERED VARIETY. Unlike most Motor Row showrooms that operated as branches of an automaker, Schillo Motor Sales at 2317–2319 S. Michigan Avenue sold a number of makes, including Mercers, Terraplanes, and Franklins. Albert G. and E.W. Schillo commissioned architects Mundie & Jensen to design the modest one-story building in 1917. The National Terra Cotta Society obviously liked the results, because it used images of the structure to promote its product. The building was vacant and padlocked in late 2020. (Photograph by John F. Hogan.)

A GOOD SPORT. One auto publication referred to the Mercer Raceabout such as this 1912 model owned by Herb Lederer as "one of the most admired sports cars of the decade." Its four-cylinder, 55-horsepower engine was capable of speeds of more than 90 miles an hour. The Trenton, New Jersey, company produced cars from 1909 to 1925. (Photograph by John F. Hogan.)

HEADLIGHTS OPTIONAL. The Saxon Automobile Company of Detroit and later Ypsilanti, Michigan, delivered a high-quality, reasonably priced line of cars that enjoyed a life span of only 10 years, from 1914 to 1923. Initially, Saxon offered a two-seat roadster with headlights optional. In 1916, two suffragettes drove a new Saxon across the country, advocating a woman's right to vote and proving the durability of the small car. They stopped in Chicago and may have visited Motor Row for service. The company later manufactured five-passenger touring cars, headlights included, guaranteed to "outperform any others in its price class [$785]." A website dedicated to the Saxon says about 100,000 of them hit the road over the company's lifespan. Its best year was 1916, when more than 27,000 were produced. (Courtesy of the William Tyre collection.)

GLASS AND CLASS. Like other Holabird & Roche designs, the Saxon building at 2313 S. Michigan Avenue relies on the copious use of plate glass on all three levels. A women's clothing and accessories shop currently does business on the ground level. (Photograph by John F. Hogan.)

A TRIO OF GEMS. Holabird & Roche reeled off three auto buildings side-by-side in the 2300 block of S. Michigan Avenue, all commissioned by attorney and real estate speculator Alfred Cowles Jr. Standing between the Saxon and Cadillac outlets, formidable company to be sure, is a showroom that Cowles reserved for himself at 2309–2311. Permits for the Saxon and Cowles buildings were issued on the same date, August 28, 1915, almost four years to the day after Cadillac got the go-ahead. (Photograph by John F. Hogan.)

EVERYTHING THAT RISES MUST CONVERGE. The Cowles building at 2309–2311 S. Michigan is a three-story brick and terra-cotta design topped in front by gently ascending steps of masonry that begin at each side and converge at the midpoint. A signature feature of a Holabird building is richly ornamental brickwork. It is not clear who the early occupants were. In late 2020, the address was an extension of the clothing shop next door. (Photograph by John F. Hogan.)

CADILLAC CORNER. The first of the Alfred Cowles Jr./Holabird & Roche collaborations, the 1911 Cadillac building fills the southeast corner of Twenty-Third Street and Michigan Avenue (at 2301–2305). In addition to the showrooms, the five-story, multi-window location contained the service department. Eight years later, the company added a building on Indiana Avenue, immediately east of the showrooms, completely dedicated to service. In the 1980s, all three Cowles buildings—Saxon, Cowles, and Cadillac—operated as a Chevrolet dealership. The original Cadillac location was renovated for condos. (Photograph by John F. Hogan.)

ANOTHER WOMAN DEVELOPER. Thomas, as in Edwin Ross Thomas of Buffalo, New York, was the name of the auto company founder. Flyer was the name of just one of a number of models the company produced between 1900 and 1919. It also built two- and three-wheel motorcycles. Nevertheless, the location at 2255 S. Michigan Avenue, across Twenty-Third Street from Cadillac No. 2, came to be known as the Thomas Flyer Garage and Service Building. It is one of the three Motor Row entries that list a woman as a developer. She was Bertha Baker Alling, a painter and wife of Van Wagenen Alling, chairman of Alling Construction Company of Chicago. The Thomas Flyer building can lay claim to at least one other distinction: it reflects the hand of two architecture firms. The original 1910 version by Holabird & Roche topped out at three stories. Five years later, two additional stories credited to Alfred Alschuler were added to accommodate a new tenant, the Chalmers Company of Detroit. At last look, the building was for lease. (Photograph by John F. Hogan.)

BELATED MOVIE FAME. The Thomas Motor Company did not survive its Chicago location for long, going out of business in 1919 after a run of less than two decades. Thomas specialized in town and touring cars. Its grandest moment of glory occurred in 1908, when its four-cylinder, 60-horsepower Model 35 won the New York to Paris Race, the only around-the-world auto race ever held. The feat inspired the 1965 movie comedy *The Great Race*, starring Jack Lemmon, Tony Curtis, and Natalie Wood. (Courtesy of the John S. Maxson collection.)

CLASSIC DETAILS, STAID NEIGHBORS. Smaller than the showroom of its competitor, B.F. Goodrich, the Kelly-Springfield Tire store at 2251 S. Michigan Avenue was designed by Alfred Alschuler in 1915. At three stories and displaying terra-cotta ornament, the building fits nicely with the auto showrooms, although an architecture critic maintains that its "large expanses of glass delicately framed by classically-detailed terra cotta" set it apart from its "staid" neighbors. At last inspection, the one-time tire outlet was looking for a lessee. (Photograph by John F. Hogan.)

Short Stay. Bearing the name of the Illinois city of its origin, the Moline Automobile Company did not get to utilize its three-story building at 2245 S. Michigan Avenue for very long. The showroom/office building went up in 1917, and the company went down in 1919. Price no doubt had something to do with Moline's demise. Its 1911 two-seat roadster sold for $1,700 while comparable makes carried tags in the $485–$650 range. Developer Edwin A. Seipp commissioned architect Howard G. Hodgkins to design the rather conventional structure. At the same time, the pair teamed up to do a building across the street at 2244 for Seipp's realty trust, apparently in expectation of leasing it to an auto dealer. That venture did not lead to any immediate occupancy, according to National Register documents. It was also looking for a lessee in 2021. (Photograph by John F. Hogan.)

TOUCH OF MIAMI. Less than eight months after it made its Motor Row debut at 2347–2351 S. Michigan Avenue, Fiat added a second, smaller building (1910) about one block north, at 2239 S. Michigan Avenue. Doing so, the company bucked two prevailing trends on the street by moving from south to north and from larger to smaller quarters. The company changed architects as well, enlisting C.W. and G.L. Rapp, who produced a small, colorful, three-story building fronted by generous amounts of plate glass. The orange and green pastels would not seem out of place in present-day Miami and work well for the contemporary occupant, the Mad Hatter cocktail lounge. (Photograph by John F. Hogan.)

AUBURN DEMONSTRATION WEEK. Shoppers gather on the sidewalk outside the Auburn showroom at 2401 S. Michigan Avenue on Motor Row to see new Auburns in action. S. Michigan Avenue, straight, wide, and level, provided an ideal place for customers to test drive new cars. (Courtesy of Chicago History Museum.)

THIRD-TO-LAST. The Cole Motor Car Company building at 2235 S. Michigan Avenue was the third-to-last district structure built, arriving in 1923. Only the second Locomobile branch (1925) and the Illinois Automobile Building (1936) were constructed later. Not much to behold originally, the one-story Cole location by architect William Whitney was a boarded-up eyesore plastered with graffiti and posters in late 2020 and was soon demolished. (National Register status typically does not prevent demolition.) The Indianapolis-based Cole Company produced high-quality luxury cars with four- and six-cylinder engines but switched exclusively to V-8s after 1916, soon after Cadillac pioneered the concept. The company shut down in 1925. (Photograph by John F. Hogan.)

AWARD WINNER. After standing vacant for many years, the Triangle Motors building underwent extensive rehab that earned it an Excellence in Preservation Award in 2019 from the Commission on Chicago Landmarks. It was an appropriate way to mark the 100th anniversary of the building at 2229 S. Michigan Avenue, which, at one time, housed an independent Ford dealership. (Photograph by John F. Hogan.)

YOUR TABLE IS WAITING. Triangle's commercial storefront was restored, masonry upgraded, missing terra-cotta replaced with replications, and glass-block windows exchanged for the double-hung variety. The final look of this three-story jewel is reminiscent of a small European opera house. Architect Lawrence Gustav Hallberg would have been proud. One cannot help but wonder what he would have thought about the new ground-floor tenant offering "the ultimate in drag dining." (Photograph by John F. Hogan.)

ON THE MOVE. The Bird-Sykes dealership, which sold cars made by a variety of manufacturers, also operated from a variety of Motor Row locations—three, to be exact. Its first building, at 2208–2216 S. Michigan Avenue, was developed by Gerabed Pushman and designed by Christian Eckstorm in 1910. It handled two short-lived makes, the Corbin, made in New Britain, Connecticut, and the Matheson, an expensive car manufactured in Wilkes-Barre, Pennsylvania. Both companies went out of business in 1912. A pizzeria was expected to move into one of the three spaces in early 2021. A bar and grill and a men's clothing boutique occupied the other spots. (Photograph by John F. Hogan.)

Exterior of the Bird-Sykes Co.'s sales and service building. This structure is being copied in many cities

THE THIRD WOMAN. In 1915, Bird-Sykes opened across the street at 2215 in another Eckstorm building. The developer is listed as Amelia Winterbotham, one of the trio of women developers of Motor Row. Her 1938 obituary somewhat cryptically identified Amelia Winterbotham as "prominent in Chicago society for many years" and the widow of John Russell Winterbotham. The building was being rehabbed for office space in late 2020. (Photograph by John F. Hogan.)

HAVE A SEAT. In 1919, Bird-Sykes opened a third location one door south, at 2221, a building it commissioned architect Harold Holmes to design. That site is now occupied by a used furniture store. (Photograph by John F. Hogan.)

BARNEY SIKES WAS EVERYWHERE. The Bird-Sykes dealership sold at least two additional cars, both headquartered in Detroit. They were the Lozier, at one time the most expensive American-made auto, and the Paige, which far outlasted the other Bird-Sykes offerings. The 1919 Paige pictured below features a golf club compartment, a door that opens behind the driver's-side door to accommodate clubs and a bag. Paige did not appeal to a broad enough market and became defunct in 1928, a total of 13 years after the Lozier. (Photograph by John S. Maxson.)

50,000 Owners Are Served Through the Bird-Sykes Organization and Its Dealers

Chicago sales field has grown into an inter-state territory, which through the parent organization and the Paige-Jewett dealers offers service to 50,000 owners.

The Bird-Sykes organization is not trustworthy because it is large and successful — it is large and successful but it has been and is trustworthy.

From the tiny store at 1040 South Michigan Avenue have grown the present properties that house the Bird-Sykes organizations in Chicago and Kansas City.

The former scantily productive

Twenty-three Years on Michigan Avenue

Not so long in the saying, but a stretch of years that is remarkable when one realizes that the motor has been with us but little more than that time.

This span of years has seen startling developments in motor cars and bewildering changes on Automobile Row. But throughout the progress of motordom, old timers will tell you that Bird-Sykes Company steadfastly adhered to its policy of trying to do the right thing.

Bird-Sykes Company

Chicago   Kansas City

FROM BIKES TO CARS. People of a certain age will remember the Nash and later American Motors Rambler from its heyday in the 1950s and 1960s. (The cars came equipped with fully reclining seats, which, according to urban legend, caused them to be banned at some drive-in theaters.) The original Rambler was the brainchild of bicycle manufacturer Thomas B. Jeffery of Chicago, who built his first car in 1897. Jeffery bought an old bike factory in Kenosha, Wisconsin, in 1900 and started mass producing cars like this 1909 model. By the end of 1902, Jeffery was turning out 1,500 vehicles, purportedly one-sixth of the total US automobile population. That scale made the company the nation's second-largest auto manufacturer, trailing only Oldsmobile. (Courtesy of Library of Congress.)

INTRODUCING THE STEERING WHEEL. Rambler introduced the steering wheel to replace the tillers found on early cars. It was also first to offer a spare tire/wheel assembly. "The car for country roads" became part of Nash Motors Company in 1917. The Mundie & Jensen–designed building from 1911, at 2246–2258 S. Indiana Avenue, remained vacant in early 2021 and in need of a facelift. (Photograph by John F. Hogan.)

MORE THAN CARS. Old murals throughout the Motor Row District are reminders that businesses in the area sold more than cars. Parts, accessories, and service attracted customers from across the region. (Photograph by John S. Maxson.)

CHILD'S PLAY FOR KAHN. The six-story, reinforced-concrete building at 2300–2308 S. Indiana Avenue was one of four built that year on Wabash or Indiana Avenues that were not directly related to the sale of automobiles. The premises were taken over later by a Chevrolet dealership, a Chrysler-Plymouth-Jeep service center, then vacated and put up for sale. The last vestige of Chrysler-Plymouth was visible in mid-2021 during the erection of scaffolding. Impressive as the Cadillac Service Building was, the project was a minor opus for the man regarded as the foremost industrial architect of his day. Albert Kahn had already designed the Packard factory in Detroit as well as Ford's half-mile-long River Rouge operation in nearby Dearborn, the largest manufacturing complex in the world at that time. (Photograph by John F. Hogan.)

STILL HERE. The first Cole Motor Car Company location in Chicago, at 2326–2228 S. Indiana Avenue, has outlasted its successor, which was demolished in late 2020. Cole No. 1 dates to 1915, eight years before the company opened in a smaller space at the more prestigious address of 2235 S. Michigan Avenue. The now-vacant four-story Indiana Avenue building was designed by architects Z.T. and C.G. Davis. (Photograph by John F. Hogan.)

ANOTHER NON-CONTRIBUTING STRUCTURE. Almost nothing is known about this four-bay garage at 2312–2324 S. Indiana Avenue, immediately south of the Cadillac Service Building and across the street from McCormick Place West. Meyer Both is listed as developer, and contractor W.J. Summerbelle wore a second hat as an architect, but only for the first of the separate entries (at 2312 S. Indiana Avenue). The division of addresses appears odd, because the building looks to be contiguous. The Both-Summerbelle construction permit was issued in 1910, but for what? The present structure appears to be of much later vintage. No date, developer, or architect is mentioned in connection with the second entry (2312–2324 S. Indiana Avenue). Like some other locations, the primary purpose of these two seems to be maintaining the continuity of the historic block. (Photograph by John F. Hogan.)

CHALLENGE ACCEPTED, MR. WINTON. If James Packard and Alexander Winton had not gotten into a furious argument in 1899, chances are the iconic Packard Motor Company would not have been born—or at least not become one of the world's foremost producers of automobiles. Mechanical engineer Packard had bought one of the first 20 cars built by Winton's company but was not pleased with all of the features. He offered Winton some ostensibly constructive suggestions for improvement, which the fledgling automaker ignored and possibly took the wrong way. That was when the discussion became heated, with the flinty Scot telling Packard, in so many words, that if he was so smart, why did he not build a car of his own? Packard accepted the challenge, and before the year was out, Winton had a competitor in the marketplace of high-priced luxury autos. (Photograph by John S. Maxson.)

Packard-Kahn Combine. With the addition of Henry B. Joy of Detroit as a major shareholder, James Packard was joined by his brother William and their partner George Weiss in forming their company in Warren, Ohio. The automaker soon moved to Detroit, where, in 1903, it began construction of a 40-acre factory complex, a colossal undertaking that early in the industry's evolution. The architect was Albert Kahn, who, 16 years later, would design Packard's impressive showroom building at 2355 S. Michigan Avenue, on the northeast corner of Twenty-Fourth Street and Michigan Avenue. That building was demolished in the 1970s and is presently a parking lot. At year's end of 2020, the former Packard warehouse at 2338–2342 S. Indiana Avenue (shown in this picture), the work of Mundie & Jensen, was being transformed into a condo building. The city had posted restrictions pertaining to landmark status. (Photograph by John F. Hogan.)

Surviving the Depression. By the 1920s, Packard was the number-one producer of luxury cars in the United States, and it was the only independent maker of such cars to survive the Depression. By the 1950s, however, Packard was falling out of favor with younger consumers and could no longer compete against the larger-scale production, mass marketing, and gigantic dealer networks of Ford, Chrysler, and General Motors. Packard purchased Studebaker in 1954 to form the Studebaker-Packard Corporation, and the Packard line of cars was discontinued after 1958. The 1956 Packard-built Clipper owned by Bruce W. Grabenkort is an example of the company's strong effort to sustain operations through the 1950s. (Photograph by John S. Maxson.)

EVERYONE WANTS A PIECE OF THE PIE.
During the early 1900s, the automobile
industry attracted so much attention and
so much money was being spent on cars
that novel advertisements appeared. This
example shows an attempt by Wilson &
Co. of Chicago to promote its "curled hair"
in an automobile's seat cushion as the
way to achieve the most comfortable ride.
(Courtesy of the William Tyre collection.)

BETTER LATE THAN NEVER. The Harold A. Howard building at 2234 S. Wabash Avenue, designed
by W.L. Stebbings in 1919, apparently was another of those unable to find a tenant early on. Since
buildings on Wabash and Indiana Avenues primarily housed automotive support operations such
as garages, service centers, and warehouses, it is likely that the Howard building was intended
for such use. Better late than never, the space is occupied by an auto repair shop. (Photograph
by John F. Hogan.)

IMAGES ON PARADE. Immediately east of the auto repair shop, between Wabash and Michigan Avenues, the city has dressed up a cyclone fence bordering a vacant lot with a row of large tarp-like images of the cars that once roamed the neighborhood. Some of the images are marred by graffiti. (Photograph by John F. Hogan.)

CHRISTIAN ECKSTORM'S FINALE. The Oneida Truck Company building rates two entries in the official Motor Row lineup because it is an L-shaped arrangement at the northeast corner of Twenty-Third Street and Wabash Avenue. On the Twenty-Third Street side (60 East) stands one of a handful of off–Michigan Avenue sites still engaged in the automotive business, the repair shop South Loop Auto Service. The section at 2247 S. Wabash Avenue, also one-and-a-half stories, was occupied by a painting and decorating concern. The Oneida buildings from late 1919 were the last of Christian Eckstorm's 12 contributions to Motor Row. (Photograph by John F. Hogan.)

CAR COMPANY MINUS CARS. Almost nothing is known about the Randolph Motor Car Company except that it "was organized in Chicago late in 1908 with a Capital stock of $300,000 for the manufacture of automobiles and accessories," according Beverly Rae Kimes in the *Standard Catalog of American Cars 1805–1942*. Kimes doubts that the company ever built a car. Historian Joynt speculates that Randolph ended up selling accessories at 2241–2245 S. Wabash Avenue, which is currently occupied by an internet communications company. (Photograph by John F. Hogan.)

CHICAGO CALLING. The four-story office building by Holabird & Roche at 2211–2215 S. Wabash Avenue is one of the few structures in the district not built for auto-related use. Constructed in 1915 for the Chicago Telephone Company, it has been called the Illinois Bell Telephone Company Building since 1920 to reflect a corporate name change. Illinois Bell later became part of AT&T. (Photograph by John F. Hogan.)

Chicago Landmark

White Castle #16
Lewis E. Russell (with Lloyd W. Ray, construction
superintendent for the White Castle System of Eating
Houses, Inc.), architect
1930

This tiny white glazed-brick building remains the best-surviving
example in Chicago of the buildings built by the White Castle
System of Eating Houses, Inc., a trailblazing, American fast-food
company that popularized hamburgers in the 1920s. This
"programmatic" building, with its unusual corner tower and
medieval-inspired crenellation, served as a "billboard" for White
Castle, visually emphasizing the company's self-proclaimed
virtues of permanence and cleanliness.

Designated on October 5, 2011
Rahm Emanuel, Mayor

Commission on Chicago Landmarks

WINGS TO GO. Chef Luciano's chicken restaurant anchors the square block at the northwest corner of Wabash Avenue and Cermak Road, at 2209 S. Wabash/43–51 E. Cermak, the way Golden Pond does one block east at Michigan Avenue and Cermak Road. The two "non-contributing" sites lend balance to the Motor Row map but had no connection to the automobile business. (Photograph by John F. Hogan.)

ONCE THERE WERE SLIDERS. Chef Luciano's is, however, historically significant in another regard. In 2011, it became a City of Chicago landmark because of its previous ownership. "This tiny white-glazed building," according to the plaque outside, "remains the best surviving example in Chicago of the buildings built by White Castle . . . the company that popularized hamburgers in the 1920s." (Photograph by John F. Hogan.)

Three

OPEN ROAD AHEAD

Many of the manufacturers and dealers that played important parts in Motor Row's development are not represented in the National Register for the logical reason that their buildings have been razed. Some, at least, get a second chance at recognition in the following chapter. Meanwhile, the City of Chicago and individual investors foresee S. Michigan Avenue as a shopping, dining, and entertainment district that preserves the automotive theme. The city has spent $10 million to upgrade the streets, sidewalks, and curbing, but the jury is still out on the neighborhood's future. While the former dealerships are a delight to behold, many await repurposing. Nevertheless, the neighborhood is worth a visit. It is accessible by public transportation and easily enjoyed on foot. In the summer of 2021, Glessner House in the nearby Prairie Avenue Historic District introduced guided walking tours of Motor Row. The ambitious visitor could tour both of these underappreciated sites in less than a day. Dead or alive, the following chapter mentions some Motor Row sites not in the National Register.

EARLY ARRIVAL. Success came early to the Winton Motor Carriage Company, the brainchild of Scottish bicycle maker and Cleveland transplant Alexander Winton. The company was one of the earliest to expand to Chicago with a dealership at Fourteenth Street and Michigan Avenue. Like all of the very earliest cars, Winton featured spoke wheels, said to be the legacy of the bicycle makers who led the way into the horseless carriage era. (Photograph by John F. Hogan.)

MORE MOVIE FAME. Winton catered to upscale consumers, selling sedans, town cars, and limousines while steering away from sporty models. Limiting its appeal probably helped induce the sales decline that ended Winton's tenure as an automaker in 1924. However, the company continued as a builder of diesel engines. Of interest to movie buffs, actor Steve McQueen drove a stolen Winton across daunting country roads in the 1969 film of William Faulkner's *The Reivers.* (Courtesy of the John S. Maxson collection.)

DON'T CALL IT A STANLEY STEAMER. The most memorable steam-powered car was the Stanley, commonly known as the Stanley Steamer, a name not appreciated by the Stanley Motor Carriage Company of Watertown, Massachusetts, or its latter-day devotees. With many fewer moving parts than a gasoline-powered car, superior performance, the ability to burn lower-quality fuel, and no cranking to start the engine, steam-powered cars were popular during the early days of motoring. Stanley continued to make steam vehicles until its demise in 1924. (Photograph by John Maxson.)

FROM STEAM TO TEAMS. Stanley operated a Chicago dealership in a now-demolished building at 2101 S. Indiana Avenue. The location is now the site of Wintrust Arena, home of DePaul University and Chicago Sky WNBA basketball teams. (Photograph by John F. Hogan.)

National Silent Power

Third Series of Twelves
A NEW MODEL

National built motors have always been abreast, and generally ahead of the industry. When four cylinders were the proper thing, National built the world's Champion Fours. When sixes came into vogue, it was National that built the first American Sixes and National Sixes of today are the highest development of that type. National was a pioneer in the latest type motor—the Twelve Cylinder.

National Twelve Cylinder cars are today in operation in every state in the Union and in eleven Foreign countries. Owners everywhere testify to the success of the Twelve.

The same corps of engineers who have produced previous successes, have within the last year, concentrated on improvements for this third National Twelve.

NEW FEATURES

Removable cylinder heads to facilitate cleaning and inspecting.

Increased size of cylinder with corresponding increase in power.

Balanced crankshaft—another power increasing improvement.

Heated intake manifold to handle effectively the low grade fuel.

Larger main bearings reduce the vibration in a practically vibrationless motor.

Valves on outside of V continued together with new design valve lifters make National Twelves most accessible of all V motors.

Independent electrical units—Delco for Ignition and separate, independent Starting and Lighting units.

¶ This new Twelve is the last word in multi-cylinder efforts to achieve perfection.

¶ From low to high speed—and at every stage in between—there is the same *high pressure* of power, even, supple and subject to your perfect control.

¶ In short, it is a marvelous motor—not to be appreciated until driven.

¶ To be the National dealer is not only to have the best motor to demonstrate, but to have the best of everything to offer customers.

HIGHWAY TWELVE $2150   **HIGHWAY SIX $1750**

12 Cylinder **$2150**   **AMERICAS BEST LOOKING CARS**   **6** Cylinder **$1750**

National Motor Car & Vehicle Corp., Indianapolis
Seventeenth Successful Year

FILL 'ER UP, CHARGE 'ER UP. For a brief time early in its existence—from 1903 to 1905—the National Motor Vehicle Company of Indianapolis offered customers a choice between electric and gasoline-powered vehicles. National began life in 1900 with a tiller-steered, nine-horsepower electric runabout whose top speed was 15 miles an hour. Three years later, the company introduced four-cylinder internal combustion cars and then dropped the electrics in 1905. In the years prior to World War I, National moved up to six- and twelve-cylinder models, but wartime inflation forced the company to price itself out of its traditional market, and it went out of business in 1923. (Courtesy of the William Tyre collection.)

EX-SHOWROOM PIZZERIA. National shared showroom and garage space with the Inter-State Motor Car Company at 1354 S. Michigan Avenue, the northwest corner of Fourteenth Street and Michigan Avenue, less than a block north of the Ford location. The imposing six-story gray building, still standing, resembles a bank. The pizza restaurant on the ground floor, where the cars were displayed behind plate glass, seems out of place. Nonetheless, it is not difficult to envision the building as part of the historic district. (Photograph by John F. Hogan.)

Fully Enclosed
For Winter

Lexington MINUTE-MAN SIX CONVERTIBLE TOURING CAR **$1350**

The outward beauty of the LEX-INGTON is a fitting accompaniment of its inward excellence. A powerful, economical, comfortable, convenient, stylish car built with care by men of broad and diversified manufacturing experience. (Close to LEXINGTON are ten big factories devoted exclusively to making motor car parts—which means that LEXINGTON has all the advantages of large-scale production with none of its extravagances.)

LEXINGTON SALIENT SUPERIORITIES

Lexington-Continental Engine
Moore Multiple Exhaust System
Cut Steel Starting Gear on Flywheel
Independent Ignition, Lighting, and Starting Circuits
Double Universal Joints
Full-Floating Rear Axle with Spiral Bevel Gears
Wick Feed Oil Cups
Engine Driven Tire Pump
Double-Bulb Adjustable Head-lamps, rigidly mounted on Radiator
Largest Size Motometer
Bolted-on Tire Rack and Spare
Demountable Rim
Oil Pressure Guage
Convex Mud Guards
Genuine Leather Trimming Throughout
In addition, the regular equipment includes full-ventilating weather-stripped windshield, speedometer, electric horn, ammeter, and trouble lamp.

LEXINGTON MOTORS CHICAGO CO.
1842 MICHIGAN AVENUE   PHONE CALUMET 5789
THE LEXINGTON-HOWARD CO.   CONNERSVILLE, IND.

BIGGER, BETTER, THEN BUST. Another Indiana-based carmaker, the Lexington Motor Company rolled out a succession of increasingly larger models between 1910 and 1927. Beginning with four-cylinder runabouts and roadsters, Lexington added an array of six-cylinder vehicles that included sedans, limousines, and touring cars seating up to seven passengers. The company's best year was 1920, when it sold more than 6,000 cars. A recession in the early 1920s sent Lexington, along with a number of other automakers, into rapid decline. (Courtesy of the William Tyre collection.)

WHY THE LIBERTY WINS

The tremendous success of the Liberty stands squarely on the unusual character of the car itself—on points where it differs from and excels every other car made.

One of the most deeply significant facts about this remarkable car is that it sells best in direct comparison with other cars, and to motorists of the highest and widest experience.

You are invited to step out of any other car and into the Liberty, and compare performance in driving and riding, point for point, as the best possible demonstration of the unusual nature of the Liberty. The Liberty has set a new standard in motoring comfort, for driver and rider—a statement which is subject to proof, and which is being proved by Liberty users all over the nation.

This car was first manufactured under conditions never before paralleled in the industry. A number of the greatest minds in the automobile business came together with the avowed intention of building a moderate sized motor car which should, above all other things, serve the owner best.

So wonderfully successful were they in the attainment of this ideal that the completed car stands apart from every other car on the market in service to owners.

In the minds of this combination of men was an experience coincident with the entire growth of the automobile industry. They knew every other car—everything that had been done. They knew what to do and what not to do to attain their ideal.

They were handicapped by no manufacturing exigencies, no old equipment stood in their way to influence them contrary to their ideal. They had a clean slate and unprecedented opportunity to build a car which should omit the mistakes of others and include features never before possible.

DUBIOUS DISTINCTION. Detroit-based Liberty Motor Car Company lasted only from 1916 to 1923. It produced just one model, the six-cylinder Liberty Six. (Courtesy of the William Tyre collection.)

ITS originality of design gives it a special appeal to people of means who seek the new and individual—yet its departures from conventional design are so logical and convincing that even the most conservative will be attracted by their manifest desirability and by the thorough quality of the car as a whole.

The new Pathfinder Seven-Passenger Touring Roadster as the most talked-of car in America, presents a new opportunity for capable dealers to enter successfully into a field hitherto closed to them.

Though the Pathfinder is now represented in a majority of the large cities, we can take care of about fifty additional dealers and shall be glad to present the Pathfinder in detail to dealers where we are not now represented.

THE PATHFINDER COMPANY
INDIANAPOLIS, U. S. A.

TO RUSSIA WITH LOVE. The influential businessmen who introduced the Pathfinder in 1912 discovered a highly unusual marketing niche: their primary market in the days prior to World War I became tsarist Russia. The war closed this export opportunity, but Pathfinder continued to make handsome, durable autos with four-, six-, and twelve-cylinder engines. However, a shortage of materials caused by the war seriously hindered production, and the company folded after only five years. Its Indianapolis factory was acquired by a shoe polish manufacturer. (Courtesy of the William Tyre collection.)

STUDEBAKER A MAGNET. The former 10-story Studebaker building at 625 S. Wabash Avenue acted as a magnet for early car dealers. While not an automaker or seller (yet), the carriage builder attracted neighbors who thought Studebaker customers might also want to take a look at the horseless variety. (Courtesy of the John S. Maxson collection.)

ROLLING TIRES TO ROLLING STONES. Some tire companies on Motor Row were more equal than others in the apparent judgment of the landmark authorities. B.F. Goodrich and Kelly-Springfield are official members of the fraternity. The more modest McNaul Tire Company building at 2120 S. Michigan Avenue did not make the National Register list, but its latter-day successor, Chess Records, has achieved far greater fame. From the mid-1950s to the mid-1960s, the one-time tire store was a recording studio that became a mecca for legendary blues and early rock 'n' roll musicians. Chuck Berry, Willie Dixon, Muddy Waters, and Bo Diddley were among the many who recorded here. The Rolling Stones visited in 1964 during their first US tour and left behind a piece appropriately titled "2120 South Michigan Avenue." (Photograph by John F. Hogan.)

SINGIN' THE BLUES. The former McNaul building is currently occupied by Willie Dixon's Blues Heaven Foundation. Garden space named in honor of the late bluesman is located next door. Though bypassed at the national level, the building was declared a Chicago landmark in 1990 but only in honor of its music fame—apologies once again to McNaul. (Photograph by John F. Hogan.)

LAST OF AN ERA. The imposing Kent House at 2944 S. Michigan Avenue is the last remaining mansion of the pre–Motor Row era, and dozens of others like it were demolished to make way for auto showrooms. Built in 1883 (over 20 years before the first dealership on Motor Row), the firm Burnham & Root designed the Queen Anne–style home for Sydney A. Kent, president of the Chicago Packing and Provisions Company. The privately owned building is a City of Chicago landmark. (Photograph by John S. Maxson.)

SHELBY APARTMENTS FITTING IN NICELY. The looks of the Shelby Apartments at 2300 S. Michigan Avenue can be deceiving; the building appears right at home on Motor Row, like a former auto warehouse. Even though the Shelby resembles the Mitchell building down the street, try finding it in the roster of landmark buildings. It is not there because the Shelby was constructed in the early 2000s, modern in every way, an asset to the neighborhood, but a building with no past on a street dedicated to the past. (Photograph by John F. Hogan.)

Washington Too. The automobile row concept was not unique to Chicago. Other cities had similarly dedicated streets, but nearly everyone agreed Chicago's were the most extensive. (Courtesy of Library of Congress.)

Successor Dealers. The Near North Side intersection of Clark and Maple Streets provides a bit of a throwback to the way things used to be. Three of the four corners are home to modern dealerships that offer cars behind large plate glass windows. (Photograph by John F. Hogan.)

WAITING, HOPING. As 2021 progressed, long after the last car had been sold, Motor Row was still in search of a repackaged identity. Like several other Chicago neighborhoods, rumors of its turnaround have been greatly exaggerated. The advent of the COVID-19 pandemic did not do much to reduce activity because there was not much beforehand, particularly in the heart of the district, from Cermak Road (Twenty-Second Street) to the start of the Stevenson Expressway overpass at Twenty-Fourth Place. (Photograph by John F. Hogan.)

LOOK CLOSELY. Art Deco banners hanging from a few lampposts bear an image of the type of classic automobile that once ruled these streets, but further indicators are few, with one exception being a plaque identifying the building at 1925 S. Michigan Avenue as the one-time B.F. Goodrich showroom, as well as a couple of signpost maps and the tarps on Twenty-Third Street. And then there are the names—Buick, Locomobile, Marmon, Premier—built into the facades of their former premises. The stretch where test drivers behind the wheels of Saxons and Maxwells and Speedwells once zipped by now sees few cars and fewer pedestrians. (Photograph by John F. Hogan.)

THE BEHEMOTH TO THE EAST. Looming immediately east of Motor Row, the McCormick Place exhibition behemoth has been the longtime home of the annual Chicago Auto Show, the largest in the nation. Thousands of auto enthusiasts from throughout the Midwest travel to attend the auto show, generally unaware that their destination is a historical setting on the brink of expanding to meet their needs for dining and meeting space. (Photograph by John F. Hogan.)

COME TO THE CABARET. Attractions are starting to appear. One is Revel Motor Row, the special events venue that occupies the Moorish-design former *Chicago Defender* newspaper building. Another is the Bassline craft brewery and taproom. There are two additional bars, the Burger King, and the eye-catching restaurant Lips, which offers "the Ultimate in Drag Dining." The front windows feature sets of cartoonish lips, flaming red and coated with as much lipstick as the law allows. (Photograph by John F. Hogan.)

Awaiting the "Explosion." Motor Row is "an interesting area that hasn't exploded," in the words of a Chicago journalist who keeps a close watch on the real estate market. The boom that the South Loop experienced has not extended to the heart of the row, but alderwoman Pat Dowell, whose Third Ward encompasses the area, sees a glass half full. "Motor Row has not reached its full potential as a viable commercial corridor focused on music and entertainment," Dowell concedes, "but still holds the promise for a bright future and is slowly coming back to life." She points to the brewery and taproom, retail stores, and event spaces along with some residential use. The city has invested $10 million in streetscaping that includes fresh pavement, widened sidewalks, and new curbing. (Photograph by John F. Hogan.)

New Neighbors? To the south, far grander projects have been proposed, but any spillover benefits—assuming the plans even materialize—face a formidable barrier in the Stevenson Expressway. In July 2021, the city announced plans to sell the nearby 49-acre site of the former Michael Reese Hospital to a private developer who intends to create, among other elements, a major Israeli medical center with plans for a multibillion-dollar research facility. Other developers have eyed the site, including some jockeying to cash in on a comparatively new federal program that offers hefty tax breaks to encourage investment in long-neglected areas. (Photograph by John F. Hogan.)

Show Me the Money. Still another potential investor has proposed a row of skyscrapers built on a 31-acre platform above the railroad tracks west of Soldier Field. The $20-billion project, one of the largest ever proposed in the city, envisions partial funding from the state, which is already heavily in debt. Given the uncertain economy and lingering effects of the pandemic, the prospect of new development remained chancy. Even if Motor Row did acquire new neighbors, how many might come calling, and perhaps join Chicagoans who have rediscovered the locale, is impossible to predict. One can always dream. (Photograph by John F. Hogan.)

LOOK TO THE FUTURE. While some communities struggle for a new identity, Motor Row's legacy as a region for automotive pioneers will long be its calling card. When Richard Driehaus, one of the most successful businessmen and generous philanthropists in the Midwest, purchased the Marmon Building with the intent of using it as a museum for his collection of over 50 fabulous cars, it signaled critical support for Motor Row by an influential civic leader. Similarly, McHugh Construction, one of the region's premier structural concrete firms, has its corporate offices on Motor Row consistent with its mission of the "unapologetic pursuit of the extraordinary." Who knows where Motor Row would be today had not a recession dampened the residential property market and COVID-19 not closed down the convention industry. Even the tragic sudden passing of Richard Driehaus adds uncertainty. But the facts remain that Chicago's Motor Row has the architectural credentials, demographics, the economic engine of McCormick Place, and its city-center location all going for it. (Photograph by John F. Hogan.)

DISCOVER THOUSANDS OF LOCAL HISTORY BOOKS
FEATURING MILLIONS OF VINTAGE IMAGES

Arcadia Publishing, the leading local history publisher in the United States, is committed to making history accessible and meaningful through publishing books that celebrate and preserve the heritage of America's people and places.

Find more books like this at
www.arcadiapublishing.com

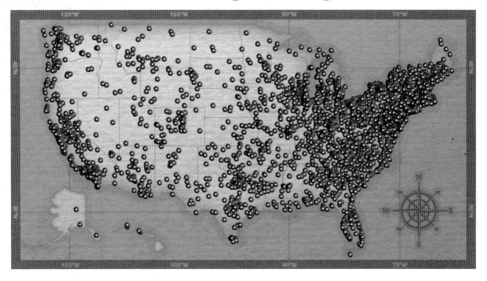

Search for your hometown history, your old stomping grounds, and even your favorite sports team.

Consistent with our mission to preserve history on a local level, this book was printed in South Carolina on American-made paper and manufactured entirely in the United States. Products carrying the accredited Forest Stewardship Council (FSC) label are printed on 100 percent FSC-certified paper.

MADE IN THE USA